CW01337854

Formby Reminiscences

by

Catherine Jacson

Centenary Edition
Facsimile reprint with extra
illustrations from
'The Formbys of Formby'

SEFTON
LIBRARIES

'Formby Reminiscences' first published 1897
'The Formbys of Formby' first published 1910
This centenary edition, limited to 500 copies,
specially produced by
Cedric Chivers Ltd., Bristol
for the publisher
Sefton Council
Leisure Services Department (Libraries),
Pavilion Buildings, 99-105 Lord Street,
Southport PR8 1RH
1997

Copyright © Sefton Libraries

ISBN 1 874516 04 9

PRINTED IN GREAT BRITAIN BY
CROMWELL PRESS LTD., WILTS.
BOUND BY CEDRIC CHIVERS LTD., BRISTOL

Foreword

To understand and appreciate a place you need to know a little of its past, the people who lived there and their way of life. What better way to understand Formby than to read the memories of Catherine Jacson. She came here many times in the early nineteenth century and, from a very early age, fell in love with the area. She described herself as 'one who had an especial sand attachment'. Her *'Formby Reminiscences'* were first published in 1897, with a second edition the following year.

Catherine was the grand-daughter of the Reverend Richard Formby of Formby Hall, who died in 1830 and is buried at St.Peter's Church. The Formbys had long been landowners in the area and their family tree can be traced back to the thirteenth century. Formby Hall has been altered many times over the years but it still stands in the woods off Southport Old Road.

Richard Formby was the Parson and Squire. He took great interest in all that was going on both in Liverpool and in Formby; and he seems to have greatly enjoyed passing on his love of the area to his grand-daughter.

If you have ever seen a picture of Formby Hall, with its walled garden and dovecote, and tried to imagine actually living there, then you will value Catherine Jacson's vivid picture of daily life in the hall. Visualise the squire sat at a table covered with estate papers and sermons, interviewing tenants and managing his estate while writing his Sunday sermon to be delivered at St.Peter's Church. He encouraged his daughters to start a village school, for local girls, in the Hall grounds. At meal times, his grand-daughter had her own dining-table in the window alcove from where – with the background of the conversation of the older generations – she could look out at the sheep and cattle in the fields.

Catherine gives us a vivid picture of walks through the woods that surround the Hall, bathing excursions at high-tide, and the abundance of wild flowers to be found on the sand-dunes. She tells us about the cows being milked and the milk going to needy villagers; about the journey to church in the family coach down sandy lanes so rough as to make the passengers feel travel sick.

Many of the pleasures of Formby that Catherine enjoyed can still be found today; the sunshine, the quiet environment and the clean sand of the dunes. Look at Formby through Catherine Jacson's eyes. Things have, of course, changed – but it is still an attractive place with its own particular charm. Sefton Libraries are to be congratulated on reprinting *'Formby Reminiscences'* with its unique contemporary illustrations.

Barbara Yorke
1997

FORMBY HALL.

FORMBY REMINISCENCES

BY THE AUTHOR OF

"DESULTORY RETRACINGS"

WITH ILLUSTRATIONS

London:

GARDNER, DARTON & CO.
3, PATERNOSTER BUILDINGS, E.C.

1897.

To the dear memories,

family and local,

of Formby in its patriarchal times.

And, especially,

To the most dear memory

of

Mary Formby,

of

Formby Hall,

These Records are tenderly dedicated.

"OUR HOUSEHOLD GODS ARE THE MEMORIES OF OUR CHILDHOOD."

PREFACE

It is a trifle more than thirty years since the chief part of these records were written. They were begun, at the suggestion of the relative to whom the first part is addressed, in the form of letters, written at once, off-hand, with a running pen, and in the warmth of a vivid loving memory, as to one who, at least in a great measure, could enter into the overflow of feeling which dictated them; and who needed no explanatory prelude as to the bearings or the ground of any seeming extravagance of description imputable to them.

As this improvised portion was first unrestrictedly written, so, untouched, it remains now in committing it to print. And this in defiance of my own suggestion, in the introductory letter, that all should, at some future time, be re-moulded into more conventional shape. I see the matter, however, now, at this more distant period, from another point of view; and judge that to attempt such a process would be but to take away all of any merit the records may possess, by robbing them of their unstudied fidelity, and, as it were, forcing the free natural flow of the rivulet into the formal bounds of the artificial lake.

But why print either these or any of the other records at all? This is a reasonable question: and, all the more so, as they bear no historical value, have no political interest, illustrate no names famous in discovery or in literature—in short, have no claim to attention on any public ground whatever.

I can but reply, first, that what constitutes individuality of character of a nature to awake interest or response in ourselves, is independent of celebrity, and is, perhaps even more, readily developed in the quieter recesses of private life, than among the competitive multitudes that crowd the highways to metropolitan distinction.

But that is not my real reason for giving these memories a more lasting form than the evanescent one of manuscript—it is only the sanction for acting on the real reason.

I have long desired, but, latterly, have come to the resolve, to offer some memorial of deeds of usefulness, and excellences of character, which it would be both ungrateful and unjust to let fall into oblivion; to say nothing of the desire to keep in memory circumstances and characteristics of times which can never repeat themselves: and I have deliberatively judged that in the pursuit of this object a faithful portraiture of the living features of a character, even if without artistic honour, is, in truth, more effective as a memorial, than the inscribing of a name on any work of art or utility of whatsoever kind—a name solely; soon to become, and remain to other generations, a name—and nothing more.

Hence the adoption of this particular manner of preserving what I wish to preserve, as far as is possible, in a life-like form. And this conclusion of mine, I discover with satisfaction, may call in the support of a strong name; as it may be said, not inaptly, to run in a parallel line with Carlyle's sentiment that "human portraits, faithfully drawn, are, of all pictures, the welcomest on human walls."

It only remains, in addition, to explain that, after the earliest portion was repeated as it stood in Part I., it seemed desirable in Part II. to adopt a different form of chapter division. And, also, after some vagrant wanderings into side paths, to carry on, in solemnity of truthful tribute, the main subject through later years to its last close.

Part III. was added to convey some explanatory details, with some flitting touches on subjects of more or less general interest. And thus is my picture framed.

CATHERINE JACSON.
Lytham, (*née* FORMBY.)
May, 1897.

CONTENTS

PART I

	PAGE
LETTER I.	1
LETTER II.	13
LETTER III.	24
LETTER IV.	57

PART II

CHAPTER I.	81
CHAPTER II.	99
CHAPTER III.	118
CHAPTER IV.	126

PART III

GENERAL SUPPLEMENTARY DETAILS	143
CONCLUSION	158

"On as I journey through the vale of years
By hopes enliven'd, or deprest by fears,
Allow me, Memory, in thy treasured store,
To view the days that will return no more."
—*Southey.*

FORMBY REMINISCENCES

PART I

LETTER I

Barton Hall,
February 1st, 1867.

MY DEAR ANN,
 Considering over your request that I would put into written record those earlier recollections of Formby days we have often talked of—recollections of the old house and its inmates and surroundings in the dear old days when paved roads were unknown in the district, and railways were not even a dictionary word; when it stood so calmly alone, the all-ruling influence in all its wide surroundings—considering how best to fulfil that your request, it seems to me the simplest plan, for the present at least, would be to send to you what you may view as a rough draft, in a series of letters such as one writes with the unstudied freedom of a running pen, as in so doing I shall be free to take memories as

they flow in, without being trammelled with the restrictions of systematic arrangement or strict rules of style.

My definite recollections date from 1822. There is a still earlier period—say 1820, in which stands out one unquiet memory of dislike, resistance, and reproval; that of a child in her nurse's arms passing along the pathway from the back-yard to the stables —the child little more than a baby, the nurse dear Jane Watts. The vision is clearly before me of an undefined face of carroty complexion—that of Joe Brown the then butler, designated by the rustic folk "the waiting mon." This functionary, holding out his arms, claimed a kiss—a claim resentfully rejected by the baby pettishly twisting round on Jane's shoulder; Jane rebuked the baby in an expostulating tone for bad manners. An odd incident to remember; but the impression of mingled penitence, irritation, and puzzle as to the right and wrong of the claim and refusal, was keen, and remains inseparably blended with the aspect of those agricultural precincts, the red farm and stable building, the nearer white-washed pig-stye walls, and the atmosphere of peaceful sunshine on the breadth of green around, which we both know so well.

But the reminiscences will fairly begin with the later date, when the whole scene—the rough lawn between the beech trees in front; the sunny garden at the back, and the narrow door-way into it; the impressive shade of the wood; the deep ruts in the wide sandy lanes; the dim awe-inspiring light of the dining room; the polished floor (tempting to slide), the bittern and the other stuffed birds, and the strange pictures of the entrance hall, with the charm of its sunny bay-windowed door-way; the North room's peculiar atmosphere; the mysterious and attractive store-room with its drugs and bottles, photographed themselves on the ductile brain of four years and three months' formation.

The dining room at that time seemed ever tenanted by a presence beyond my ken in its altitude, that of my grandfather* with powdered head, and knee buckles, and abundant converse always removed far above the stretch of my understanding; all inspiring me with silent awe, and an unenquiring reverence.

The North room had a feminine dignity more approachable. There, deference and a certain marvelling observancy yet permitted some degree of childlike familiarity, and even of sport at times; but undeniably those earliest days have more depth and gravity than joyfulness in their associations. This would be owing no doubt to my own shyness, and to the ever present anxiety to fulfil the maternal charge, " not to be troublesome," as also to the constant presence of old people, as of course I then conceived all there to be.

Yes, there was certainly somewhat of pressure in those earliest days. A little lonely visitor, and having neither nurse nor playfellow, I must have been, no doubt, rather a charge to my aunts; not as being difficult to manage, but as being ever on their hands. At the 5 o'clock dinner hour I was appointed to sit in the dining room at the table in front of the window, on which stood then, as in later days, the leather blotting book and the inkstand, which were ever a part of the room's furniture. A slate was given me for my delectation on which I clearly remember trying to depict the sheep and lambs on the uncut lawn, or the rooks as they mustered in large flocks on the trees, with their evening clamour, so interwoven with these memories. How well I can recall looking through first one and then another

* The Rev. Richard Formby, LL.B., born 1760.

of the diamond panes of that thick mullioned window, now at one sheep or bird, and now at another, and making a picture border of the frame, all to help on the onerous time of that still-sitting during the long dinner hour when all were talking wisdom so high and, in its effect, somewhat depressing as so far removed from aught I knew of. A child so situated has unconsciously a sense of being beyond sympathy, and of being, in fact, without the pale of humanity. A sense of uneasiness, which I so account for, has impressed those prolonged hours so clearly on memory's eye, that I now see and hear the rooks, the slow movement of the pasturing sheep with the occasional plaintive bleat, and the flow of that conversation which I was so unable to follow.

The Sunday of that period too stands out before me. There was the school, then the mere shed behind the garden wall, to which I went with my aunts now and then, with too much of a scholar's feeling to take genuine delight in it. There was even then the early breakfast in the North room for the three aunts (I think by turns, not all together). In that North room I was on one of these Sundays called upon by my Aunt Mary to repeat the parable of the Good Samaritan to the curate (I think Mr. Hodgson) who had on some unwonted business come over in the early morning, and the awe of such divinity examination, with the trembling anxiety to get through it without a break-down, has given me a sympathy with all candidates for public awards from Sunday scholars upwards.

More clear still is the drive to church in the old yellow family coach of those days (before the invention of the notable two-wheeled chaise) ploughing at foot pace steadily through the deep sand, and heaving from side to side with the rolling motion of

MULLIONED WINDOW IN DINING ROOM.

THE DRIVE TO CHURCH

a vessel at sea; with closed window, or windows, too, as my grandfather feared draughts. I, placed bodkin between my two aunts, so as not to incommode my grandfather, have wonderingly watched him overlooking his sermon; and, very shortly beginning to feel at each heave of the carriage an increasing sickness, and in terror of consequences foreseen, have in truth had occasion enough to retain a keen recollection of the early discomforts of those old deep-rutted sand roads, so dear as they were to the free footstep, or the saddle of later days.

On one fatal Sunday I succumbed to these influences, and, turning no doubt a very white face to my aunt, asked in trembling haste to be put out. At this moment I can picture to myself our Aunt Ann's perplexed concern; and I conjure up her anxious countenance divided between her sympathy for a little suffering frightened child, and her distress and vexation that her father should be exposed to inconvenience, or interrupted in his reflections by the ungainly mischance of an insignificant urchin. I do not positively remember the look and manner, but my then painful sense of misdemeanour, my shame and distress at the disturbance thus made, reveal it all to me.

I do not doubt that it was this singularly devoted solicitude of all my aunts for their father's slightest comfort; their ever anxious watchfulness for the faintest expression of his wish; their unbounded devotion and veneration, shewing itself even in the most casual speech in reference to him,—it was, I doubt not, the grave impression all this made on my spirit which engendered the feeling of awe with which I regarded my grandfather. His manner to me might well have won a tenderer feeling, for it was ever kind, cheerful, and even playful, and it had a courteous charm by which all were more or less won ; yet in my case I confess a distant reverence at this period prevailed over other feelings.

At this time the family party most clear in my remembrance consisted of my three aunts, and my Uncle Hesketh, as resident, and an occasional other uncle or two falling in temporarily,—then, too, I first remember my aunt, your mother, who so pleasantly joined with me in some diversion in which the sheep and lambs were prominently concerned.

Our Uncle Hesketh, so loved, and looked upon with such easy familiarity in later days, was to me at this time an object of terror. It was then the habit of all people to tease children, and his threat of bringing for my wearing a *blue pig-tail*, when he returned from his weekly Sunday duty in Liverpool, was a source of horror to me of which I am sure he had no notion. It haunted me by day and by night; probably from the ingrained aversion I had to the pig tribe, most especially when dead ; and a " pig-tail " was to me in those days the veritable tail of a pig. Our Aunt Ann's playful threat of putting a large stone on my head that I might never grow any taller, also lay upon me with the weight of a real stone. Of the misery of this apprehension she also fathomed little. As to our Aunt Bessy, something as much like warfare as was consistent with general subservience on my part, subsisted between us—she, being then quite youthful, took an honest delight in unmitigated straightforward teasing.

From this period dates the growth of my life-long love for my Aunt Mary. The one chief delight that then over-ruled all others was an occasional hour with her on the Bronc,* where, seated above a rabbit hole, she initiated me in the delights of making thimble and cockleshell pies of the damp sand which

* A rabbit-warren so named.

we scratched up from below, dusting them well with the dry, and putting them on a piece of broken slate in the rabbit hole to bake. So superlative was the delight of this process that I remember it was a perplexity to me that one of my Aunt Mary's standing, able to do as she pleased without asking leave, should not, every day and evermore, be on the Bronc, and engaged in such a soul-entrancing enjoyment.

The period of this first well-remembered stay was, I have been told, a month. I should have supposed it much longer. There was a question, I conclude, of extending it; for I was one day summoned at an unwonted hour into my grandfather's presence, and being perched on a chair before the table at which he was sitting, was questioned, most courteously I am sure, as to my own sentiments relative to the proposed extension. The scene rises before me : my own painful perplexity ; the longing for home, and the sinking of heart at the prospect of prolonged terrors and repression, yet the shrinking from what intuitively seemed the rudeness of saying I wanted to go. Wriggling in the torture of the moment, my feet encountered the leg of the dining table at which both I and my grandfather were sitting; it at once suggested a compromise. With a very red face, I am confident, and with a trembling voice, I suggested that Jane would very likely want me at home, " to help her to rub the table legs," an office which, in fact, I had very often performed with considerable satisfaction under her supervision.

My grandfather evidently at once saw through the subterfuge, and understood the struggle and the childish delicacy, in which he probably recognized an off-shoot of his own especial characteristic. He got up hastily, stroked down my small head with his two hands, repeating with his animated emphasis,—

"You are a *very* good little girl, a VERY good little girl," increasing the stress on the adverb in the repetition.

I do not remember his other words, only that they went to establish my return as originally contemplated. Bewildered by the unexpected praise, relieved and reassured; grateful, yet with an uneasy sense of perplexity underlying, the vivid impression of this scene swallows up all the remainder. I remember neither the departure, nor the arriving home; and my life for a space melts into indistinctness.

Strange the attraction of the place notwithstanding this desire of release. Strange the depth and power of that love that has bound my heart to it from the time of this my first dawn of memory.

I do not know how many times I revisited it again between this date and the return from our first journey into France; but, prior to that, I recall the secret joy when an excursion was proposed from Orrell, where we then lived, to the Lions of the Ince entrance gates, about half-way on the road to Formby, and the secret thrill of hope that by some unknown contingency, by some means which experience had not then proved illusory, we might be led on to find ourselves there. "Our beautiful house," as my brother Henry and I then called it in confidential talk. A well-proportioned, battlemented white pile standing sun-lit between the two dark flanks of trees, its calm and simple beauty had it seems even then entered into our natures. How often since, and how tenderly, has it impressed me both in sight and memory! and what a yearning of heart was it wont to stir as the stillness of its solitude, and the witchery of its sunshine, would rise in later childhood to the mental eye in the "tracasseries" of the Champs Elysées, or the turmoil of Regent Street.

THE HOUR ON THE SOFA

Belonging to the four-year-old memories is the long length of a probationary hour spent on the sofa in the North room, which a partial leaning to the childish days moves me to add.

I had been I conclude with my Aunt Mary alone, but memory only begins with a summons which took her hastily away. On leaving the room she lifted me on to the sofa with a charge not to move from it till her return; given probably with a view to keep me safe from the fire.

I had no measure of time then; but I have been told that the period was really more than an hour. How shall I attempt to describe its long-protracted silent length?—the first few moments of patience, then the wistful listening for a returning step, then the devices to beguile the weary minutes—that well-known sofa, then ample and commodious in its old-fashioned dimensions, was afterwards divided into two couches. In its earlier more comfortable form it stood against the wall opposite the window. Over it, precisely in the middle, hung a thermometer in a red case within reach of touch; above that, and on each side of the sofa, beyond reach, hung well-known pictures. The sofa was provided at each elbow with a bolster, as was the custom of its era. To get upon one of these bolsters and then travel to the other and stand upon that,—this was the first plan of action, improved upon presently by making a stage at the thermometer mid-way, and there trying to find some interest in its mysterious lines and figures, and even venturing to touch with the tip of a finger its red leather case. This course having been carried out to weariness was relieved for awhile by the variety of tracing the flowers on the pattern of the sofa-cover with an imaginary pencil. Then in the great poverty of resource, the journeys were resumed in increasing weariness, broken with intervals of eager expectant listening at approaching steps, followed each time by the heart sickness of deferred hope as they passed by hastily towards the store-room.

But the longest hour comes to an end, and at last, at last, the door handle was touched; and oh! relief, and consolation, and speedy forgetfulness of the hour of affliction! Aunt Mary returned in much kindly concern for her little charge whom, and whose circumscribed limits, she had forgotten in the surprise and alarm attending a prolonged and dangerous fainting fit of one of the servants to whom she had been called to minister.

Finding her little prisoner with an honest, if a somewhat troubled countenance, faithfully wearying within the prison bounds, and touched perhaps with the joy that bubbled up on the release, she said words of commendation, indicative too of some surprise that the little forgotten solitary had not taken measures to find some one of whom to enquire into reasons and causes.

I remember my own answer—" But you said I was to stay on the sofa till you came back"—and the inward feeling of perplexity as to how that clear injunction could be reconciled with the implied expectation that I should have gone out of the room to look for somebody, which must necessarily have involved a getting down from the sofa.

Simple but direct references to a moral law of right and wrong such as this, and others I could bring forward, suggesting themselves thus in the early dawn of thought, not only apart from all teaching of the schools, but antecedent to the power of clothing the inward feeling with words, may they not plead for the doctrine of innate perception, and of a law of conscience, which some systems of philosophy refuse to recognize?

THE PINNACLE OF GLORY

I do not recall with any clearness the intermediate visits that must have taken place between this first four-year-old Formby memory and our first going to France two years afterwards. One day of great glory is however very clear to me, though I cannot fit it exactly into its right framework. At Orrell, in the days when my brothers sat on the nursery chest of drawers, and drove the four nursery chairs with triumphant effect, it was the cherished desire of my heart to be a carter; and I appropriated one chair newer than the others as my one cart-horse, not presuming to aspire to the inaccessible dignity of the coach-box and four-in-hand.

Now it came to pass in one of these not well defined intermediate visits, that, by means and chances that have melted away beyond recall, I found myself in Edward Aindow's company. Edward was the coachman, and the horses being most rarely wanted on other days than Sundays, he and they were often employed on week-days in light farm work. Edward had once or twice put me on Boxer's back in the stable, and he was therefore much my friend. On this occasion, by chances and means unrecalled, I fell in with him when out with both horses in the cart, Gamester in the shafts as was his wont, and Boxer leading; and with infinite delight, undisturbed by any misgivings as to propriety, I joined the trio. Historical truth rigidly compels me to confess that the cart was taking out manure. The meadow that was to receive it was close to the back entrance gate,—the water-meadow it was called. Oh! joy beyond all calculation; when there, Edward put into my hand the cart-whip, and resigned to me his office, and, taking the spade for the spreading, joined the other labourers. Then, when the enriching heaps had been laid down around, and it needed that the cart should move a few yards further, he called to me, " Now Miss Queeny ! "—a bye name of my early childhood—and I ejaculated loudly, " Boxer!" and the docile animal responded by moving on, and Gamester followed ; neither seeming in the least to despise or question the authority of their pigmy vicegerent. When they were to stop Edward called upon me again, and I ventured on that cabalistic word, " Wo-hay," which I think Edward a little assisted behind the scenes, thereby making it fully effective. Then I filled up the intervals of stoppage by rubbing down the fetlock after the approved fashion of the initiated in horsecraft, and lifting up the forefoot to examine knowingly the hoof ; and, when no one was watching, stretching on tiptoe to stroke the nose, and laying a small hand on the shoulder to feel the pleasant warmth, and recognize the proud fact that it was a real horse, and that I was a bona-fide carter.

When I returned home from this ennobling exploit overflowing with eagerness to tell of all its glories, my transport was cut short by being given to understand that distinction of that class lay beyond the legitimate aspiration of little girls, and must be foregone in future.

And thus in the early morn of life was dissipated one fond ambitious dream.

LETTER II

February 5th, 1867.

My Dear Ann,
 Pausing at the close of the first stage in these memories, I ask myself how the tale of them would be likely to tell to an uncaring ear. Would it seem a rhodomontade of fancy, or in the kindliest judgment, at best, a mere gentle fiction ? Let me protest against such a judgment. Let me at least plead for the one merit that the narrative possesses ; that it is in good faith, the simplest and most exact transcript of genuine truth. As I describe the feeling so was it felt—as I picture the object so was it then seen. I would not for anything import into the realities of the earlier vision and the young faith any ornamental fancies or mere conventional phrases of an after growth. I, telling you this my story, as from me who know to you who will believe, would desire assuredly naught to set down for effect ; neither aught to extenuate in fear of supposed exaggeration.

To resume the little history. When I had reached the more mature age of six years our home at Orrell was broken up, and my memories for the present period have to do with long days in post chaise and the mail-coach of the bye-gone time, with changing scenes in England, some winter months in Jersey, and an early spring at Dinan where was a horse fair after Rosa Bonheur's kind; then three nights and two days in a diligence to Paris, and lastly, when there, with its especial impressions of Charles Dix with white head and gentlemanly bearing, of the little boy-duke de Bordeaux, bowing from the carriage window to a sullen crowd that responded not, of the awe of the Tuileries, stately and guarded, and of the attraction of the Palais Royal, as a place of shops in which it was my delight to choose various little articles intended as souvenirs to my aunts, to be disclosed and presented in that North room, the thought of which secretly made my heart dance.

I pass over the home journey, the crossing to Dover, and six happy weeks at Fairlawn in the time of rook-shooting, cowslips, and Epsom races. But there are associations there which, if I were giving my own history, would claim a chapter to themselves. (See "Desultory Retracings.")

The mere arrival there in the dim evening light, or rather darkness, after posting rapidly from Dover, made a strong impression upon me. The rattling of the wheels on the flagged pavement before the house after the comparative silence of the macadamised drive, the light and space within, and the expectant awe of being ushered before stranger relatives, well schooled as I had been to avoid awkward blunders in the case of the one afflicted with blindness, makes the stopping of the chaise re-awake even now a not disagreeable thrill. At the actual moment it made my heart rise to my throat—but I pass on.

The memory of the actual arrival at the old Hall, on this present occasion, is not clear as that of the first stoppage at Fairlawn. What stands out most strongly is a sense of shyness at meeting my brothers, who had been left at the parsonage with Mr. Bowman, and who evidently regarded me with the masculine contempt that small school-boys entertain for smaller girls; and, also, I bear well in mind the

THE GARDEN.

surprise and disappointment at the actual size of the house. The eye that had been introduced to Palaces and Cathedrals received a shock on view of the shrunken dimensions of the place it had deemed majestic in its beauty, and had to re-adjust its measurement with some degree of mortification. It was a disappointment also (though I know not why it should have been) to find that the battlements were not chimneys—a use which the four-year old judgment had assigned to them.

But the shock and disappointment extended no further. There was still the same atmosphere in the North room, the same dim honoured light in the dining room, the same gracious presence there, with the white powdered head, the knee buckles, and the marvellous converse. There was the sunny garden stepped into from the narrow door-way, and, beyond the division of its flower borders, the shady walks under the apple trees, and all the wealth of gooseberry bushes; there was the pigeon-house and the pleasant cooing of its tenants, there was the mysterious gloom of the wood walk where the old fir trees were; and all these had an increased charm now, for the fear and pressure that had weighed on the solitariness of very tender years were removed for ever. Above all, the sandy roads were dearer; for in the interim since those days, donkeys had been added to the out-door attractions. Words would be poor indeed to represent the charm of riding with Aunt Mary to cottages, and with messages to the workpeople, or of making one of a party of mother and aunts with the grey pony to the shore for bathing.

The Grey Pony! it deserves a special introduction.

It was my grandfather's shooting cob, broad backed and stout, with hogged mane and short thick tail half a foot in length, sliced abruptly off as the fashion was then. The seat of honour in these bathing excursions was on its back, but, as a makeweight, the rider had to be cumbered with a large bundle depending from the saddle pommel and containing the bathing dresses and towels; any other smaller accessories being carried by a stout maiden on foot who always attended the caravan to open gates and serve as assistant groom and dresser.

O joys multiplied, and succession of delights!— mounting in the sunshine at the front door, passing under the shade of the drive, through the white gates, across the two fields, by the shaded farmhouse, into the sandy lane, then over the bright breezy level of the Bronc, through the rabbit gates and the green-sward passages, into that marvellous wilderness of sand hills, wending through it by landmarks not to be traced but by those to the manner born, and so on to the wide plain of shore with the ocean tide in the distance—then the disrobing in the hollow of the hills, on the dry and warm sand with the blue sky for tent above, the running, capering and laughing, in the free bathing dress, over the long stretch of untrodden shore, into the waves that broke on the sand with such a glorious roar, there splashing, ducking over head, dancing and rejoicing; then unreadily returning, but still with the happy home ride in prospect, joyously re-robing in the sand hill dell with the scream of the sea birds, and the furtive peering of a rabbit for only intrusion; remounting, and reaching the dear shades of the wood in time to be combed straight for the mid-day meal in the North room, where the luncheon tray was brought for the ladies—the tray that let its sides down in a mysterious manner, and spread itself over the table with its necessary meatdish, its charm of gooseberry tart and preserve puffs, and its jug of delicious butter-milk which it was pride to drink out of a tumbler glass and not out of a silver cup with handle. How shall the joys of these delights be adequately conveyed by description? Nay, they exceeded by their more numerous elements the extasy of the infantile hours when the utmost desire of the heart found its fulfilment in the presence of the most beloved and the baking of thimble pies.

There was no long dinner hour now to be sat through in stillness and silence, with the sheep and the rooks to mock the vain effort to portray them. That hour had now its own especial charm, for it was milking time, and with dear old Jane, (not then old) in the shippons, how over quickly the hour passed among the large herd of cows, then kept for the purpose of supplying the poorer cottagers with milk, among the calves, among the frothy milking cans, and among the milking women, with "Ailse Mackerel" at their head, in the rustic dress of linsey. How kindly was ever their welcome! for the children of the house were regarded with a respectful love and interest as in some sort belonging to all; for the spirit of clanship and of feudal or patriarchal days reigned then in that realm of pristine sand and simplicity.

What a gentle moral influence also was there ever both to giver and receiver in the visit to the cottage, and the long chat by the hearth with the aged or the invalid; the kindly enquiry, the unrestrained speech, at once respectful and affectionate, the community of interest, the bond of union in the very name—the familiar home-name of Formby.

Perhaps there was in all this some want of catholicity; the expanse and the stretch of it were not cosmopolitan. But have we really gained so much by this widening of our moral sphere, and our superiority to home-restricted affections?

There were two of these happy visits in this period, one in the summer of '25, and the other in the spring of '26; and then we took our second journey to France early in my ninth year; and I, for my part, left my heart in the sand land, with its deepest devotion silently and more especially concentrated in the halo that encircled the very name of " Aunt Mary," a name I would hardly venture but with a tender trepidation to utter aloud alone in a closed room, that I might hear the articulated sound, and seem for a moment to be speaking to her very self; and the baseless fiction would bring a quivering of heart, a mingled thrill of emotion and of pain at the unresponsive void!

Yes, the child who was too shy or too shame-faced to give utterance to the secret of the heart, has in the Paris life when secure from observation in the early night hour, re-pictured the look, the manner, the tone ; and giving way to the yearning of soul to be again in that presence, and in those scenes, in which the rides, the cows, the rabbits, the rooks, the rooms, the passages, the pictures on the walls, and the all pervading sunshine, floated in a sort of indiscriminate heaven, has, heart-sick with the hopelessness of the long distance and the little mention of return, buried a hot face in the pillow, and found relief in an outbreak of passionate grief.

To compare incongruous things, there is probably as much contrast between the decades of 1820 to 1830, and 1860 to 1870, in Paris as in Formby. At the earlier date, with the exception of the Rue de Rivoli, the Rue de la Paix, and another, the name of which I cannot now recall (Rue Casliglione), the streets were narrow, dirty, and ill-lighted, in a degree hardly credible now. The Rue St. Honoré, a main thoroughfare, was narrow and crooked all the long length, without " trottoir," with an open gutter down the middle, offensive to sight and to smell, and lighted at distant intervals with oil lamps depending over the gutter by ropes strung across from the opposite houses.

Prices also were low, and indoor life was simple, at least among the moderate classes, and, to judge by the equipages of the great, which were neither many nor well-appointed, their private life also was simple in its kind. The outdoor life, which is in fact there the life of the people, found its enjoyment in the social gatherings of numbers, in seeing and being seen; the chair hired for a sou, or the little round table with eau sucré under the tree by the summer café tent, secured a station from which to exhibit the personal toilette and to watch the gay scene around. Polichinelle, music, a tame hare with a pistol, a dancing dog, a whirl-about, news, and chatter, were the entertainments which sufficed to delight young and old in the Champs Elysées, or the Boulevards; and the public taste and the public eye were not offended with indecency and coarseness. La politesse was independent of delicacy.

For my part, though the shows and booths and the dancing dogs were not without their natural attractions, there was no moment when, had Aladdin's lamp been at my command, I would not have been borne off from all the variety and the glitter to the solitude where the white gates enclosed the home of my fathers, which was to me the pivot of the globe.

Our course was from Boulogne to Versailles for a winter, then to Paris as head quarters or home. From thence we went to St. Germains for a summer month, and to Tours by Orleans and Blois, spending a rural fortnight at Chambord in hot harvest time, the happiest fortnight of the French years—indeed a time of real child enjoyment, fishing with my brothers in the sluggish stream, defying imaginary wolves in the forest, wandering at ease over the yellow plain, and caring little for the historical associations of Francis the First, closely linked with the many-peaked château which stood neglected in its unkept grounds close to our solitary rustic auberge.

The market place at Tours deserves a passing notice from the wealth of its autumn fruits; the peaches in cart-loads, the grapes in panniers, the large pears melting like the butter which suggested their name, the figs less approved: these things, I confess, were more interesting to me than the wide flow of the Loire with its tale of revolutionary horrors, or the notable interest of its many-arched bridge. More might be said of the various quaint costumes of the peasantry which made the market places in the country towns so picturesque. They are familiar remembrances to me, as I frequented them constantly as interpreter and deputy bargainer to Jane, who made the purchases and haggled for a reduction of price in everything with a bull-dog tenacity; and not without reason, for her English face provoked cupidity.

The English at that time had not been forgiven Waterloo; and in Paris it was a common thing to be followed by a few "polissons" calling out, "Bêtes Anglaises" or "Monsieur God-dam." So much for French urbanities in 1827.

As a sketch of French habits, I will mention a kind friend of mine in Paris, one Madame de L'Or, an officer's widow, who lived above us in two rooms, au troisième, with some very tame canaries. As I remember her she was in all respects a gentlewoman. She had no servant; the porter's wife came up for half-an-hour in the morning to light the fire and do a little rubbing. She cooked her own dinner, a potage, or a fricassée, on a little portable stove the size of a flower pot, which she slipped into the bedroom if a caller came. Towards four o'clock she would go forth, well dressed, to the Tuileries or elsewhere (taking me with her at times) and sitting with a friend or acquaintance, would spend a social evening, at the cost of a sou, in the midst of the gay crowd, and fill her rôle in it as effectively as Madame la Comtesse.

I cannot take final leave of the foreign life without for a moment recalling the well-accustomed scene on the Boulevards: the "Boulevard Italien" of the old régime; the cafés with open front to the trees, and the little round tables under their shade; the stalls with their gay trifles loudly proclaimed, at "trois sous et demi," at "dix sous," at "vingt cinq sous"; the tame canary for sale perched under an archway of immortelles; the bunch of violets for a liard. Undoubtedly the tastes, pleasures, and habits of life were simpler in those years than now.

The heavy atmosphere of the hot summer's evening—how it comes back to me! with the gay idlesse of lively groups, pleased with the simple and even childish entertainments that a few sous would purchase; pleased with merely chatting one to another, and looking on—the general air of cheap enjoyment and careless mirth, how the very life of it rises before me, with that sweet impression of genuineness and stability which was ours to know when we reckoned our years by units only, and which differs from our older feelings as the warmth of the summer evening light from this grey winter gloaming!

And Félicie Karr,—what has become of Félicie, my little friend at Madame Afforty's school, where I went every other day for a few months, portfolio in hand, with Céline the porter's wife, often to be exhibited to callers and incomers as "la petite Anglaise," with the rosy cheeks and the untortured hair. "Que ces enfants Anglais sont donc des anges!" a remark frequent enough, and due no doubt to the contrast with the Parisian sallowness, and the Parisian "modes."

Opening the other day a long-closed desk, an old glass Paris bonbonière revealed itself, in which, among other greater treasures (a rose-bud from the wreath worn at Formby at the feast of the Bower, a little thread with which Aunt Mary had once tied a small parcel, and the like), a very small ill-written note appeared couched in these unscholastic words:

"Chère Amie,
    Tu m'as fait des vers. Il est juste que je t'en fasse
—Les voici,
    'Chère Amie
    Tu fais le bonheur
    De ma vie.'
Réponds moi sur du papier à lêttre.
        Ton Amie,
            Félicie."

Félicie, my little friend! I fear I have not been as faithful to that early bond as to some others. Truth to say I had forgotten all about that sweet poetic token; yet the sight of the little ill-taught scrawl touched me, and awoke a somewhat strong, though passing, longing once again to re-visit scenes unloved at the time of daily seeing, but beautified now by that glamour light of child remembrance, which converts the early realities of this our common world into a vision of sweet idlesse in which at least no darker care or toil obtruded than the sad perplexities of a long-division sum.

If I were to be nearly questioned as to the ground of this charm which is thrown over the recollections of days and scenes caught back with the very impress of the eye and mind of childhood, I should be inclined to attribute it to the unconscious fulfilment of our Lord's teaching which it is given to childhood, by nature, to carry out: the wisdom of taking no thought for the morrow,—the immunity of the lilies and the ravens from anxious care. Childhood has no pressure of thought as to future difficulty whether of food or clothing or of stature of body or mind. It toils not, neither does it spin either in hand or brain. It receives and takes note without effort. In one word it enjoys without care.

Surely the joys of the perfected spirit will have some sort of high analogy to this feature of our first beginning.

LETTER III

February 7th, 1867.

My Dear Ann,

Another era of the reminiscences dates from our return from France in 1829, in the early autumn, for I remember the vintage was going on in drenching rain, which however could not chill the rejoicing of the homeward journey. The white cliffs of Dover triumphed over the sea-sickness, and hardly I think did longing exile return to fatherland with fuller joy than did I.

We spent that winter at Walmer, where I remember the Duke of Wellington walked one morning on the beach like any ordinary mortal, having arrived at the Castle unexpectedly the night before, and relieved the old woman who was in charge by lighting his own fire, and telling her not to put herself out of the way, as an old soldier was accustomed to help himself.

The Duke was not then popular. On that morning when he was walking on the beach my father took off his hat and cheered him loudly, desiring to get up a demonstration; there were several people about, but no one responded. The Duke quietly acknowledged my father's salutation, and walked on. My mother was very indignant at the silence of the lookers on, and I could have cried over the disgrace with which her censure invested my countrymen.

THE WALMER FRIENDS

Ah! let me add also a grateful notice of good friends at Walmer—the Brooks family—the kind old gentleman and his four daughters, who let the little girl chatter to them of all her past experiences, and tell the dear tale of Formby happiness and its expected renewal, without seeming ever to weary of it; giving her welcome to the house at all times, and free access to the couch of the invalid who was, even above all the others, her kind and indulgent friend.

This theme would lead me far astray; but let me here, in one short line, record the grateful sense which mature age cherishes of the happiness and profit derived from kindness shewn in many instances to the child.

On our northward way we stayed again a week or two at Fairlawn. The spring wore itself at last into summer at Accrington, and then—then—once more to Formby, — the months, the weeks, the days, having been counted up, and checked off up to that reckoning.

Before I enter upon somewhat more mature experiences, let me, if not for your need, yet for the sake of a younger succession, describe the family as it was then. Assuredly a later generation will never see a reproduction; for the fashion of that time is past, and the die from which nature cast our two elder aunts, at least, is broken, and will not be replaced.

Our grandfather was the refined and accomplished gentleman of the old school, with manners and habits punctilious in their courtesy; and with the gift of fluency and elegance in the expression of warm and even passionate feelings, and, withal, of a very tender and affectionate heart.

His six sons, unlike himself, were cast in a large mould, all handsome men—some eminently so—in their youth strong, and reckless in daring on horse or foot, good shots, and rash in sporting adventure.

The three daughters were in the fullest sense of the word, good looking, as distinguished from the term "beautiful" in its ordinary feminine meaning. They were all tall; the two elder, Ann and Mary, were in dignity of countenance, as in character, superior to the ordinary type of womankind. I hardly like to exalt one above the other, where both were so excellent; but of our Aunt Mary it might assuredly have been pre-eminently said, "She was a woman of good understanding, and of a beautiful countenance."

> "In her had Nature bounteously combined
> The tenderest bosom with the strongest mind."

And to her had nature given the power to say the right thing at the right time, and to word it in the best way; and also the yet rarer gift of the will to make others happy in *their* way rather than her own.

Speaking generally, both were equally devoted as daughters, equally considerate as sisters, equally untiring in promoting the good, temporal, moral, and religious, of the simple population around them. Ann, the eldest of the daughters, was at all times deferred to by her sister Mary; but perhaps in general estimation she took the second place, from no real inferiority however, for perhaps hers was in reality the stronger character of the two, but from greater reserve and formality of habit, also perhaps from the effect of a pre-eminent scrupulousness of conscience, which multiplied her difficulties and anxieties in the common daily dealings of life, causing a degree of restraint in speech and action, and thus often provoking raillery from the brothers, though assuredly ever inspiring respect in all; and also (though indeed with no prejudice to this most genuine respect) often affording in reference and quotation a store of private jest and comedy to the juniors of the family, who as they grew to understand and to love the higher excellences, became also more alive to the obvious minor peculiarities of a character in which the sensitiveness of, what I may term, chivalrous delicacy and refinement combined singularly with a rigid determination in matters of principle which would, I am persuaded, have confronted, unflinching, the fires of Smithfield.

The youngest sister, our Aunt Bessy, was regarded with more familiarity, and fell more on the level of easy companionship. Her character was less distinctive than that of her elder sisters, but her more youthful tastes and presence, her gaiety, and good nature, and more blooming beauty, were an element of pleasure in the family, and had their especial share in the brightness of the home life.

The brothers being all married and dispersed at this time, the sisters take perforce the foreground in the home record.

My grandfather had made the mistake of marrying again late in life. Of Mrs. Formby (always so called) no one saw much. She sat alone in an upstairs boudoir of her own, and rarely mixed with the family party except at meals. She had literary tastes, but an unsocial and uncertain temper. She was no drawback to the enjoyment of the younger generation; but, to my aunts, the upstairs boudoir was the cupboard that contained the skeleton of the house. I am not sure that it was not in some measure so to my grandfather, but the courtesy of his nature was a bar to the most distant manifestation of such a sentiment, if such existed.

To return to the narrative. At an unwonted

morning hour, two or three days after this present happy arrival, I was sent for to speak with my grandfather in the dining room.

With a quickened circulation I obeyed the summons, and entered the presence-chamber; to me still invested with a shrouded sovereign dignity.

On the table, at which my Aunt Mary was sitting, lay a multitude of papers, a mixture of sermon sheets, and estate plans, and by it stood my grandfather who had been walking about the room, as was his custom when dictating his sermons or letters. My eye took in all these things, attention being quickened by expectancy. My grandfather advanced to meet me with a courtesy and punctilio that in these days would hardly be bestowed on a person of distinction; and after a few questions, and a slight preface, made me understand that there was a certain farmer, John Bond by name, who had a pony—a pretty pony—a small pony—a pony in all points suitable for a small horse-woman, and that he had little doubt arrangements were possible by which the small pony might be made virtually mine for the time being, if that was a plan that would be agreeable to me. I don't know how I may have answered, but my grandfather was evidently satisfied that the plan would be agreeable, unequivocally, and in no ordinary degree.

"Then, if Mary will be good enough to see John Bond to-morrow?" said he, turning enquiringly towards my Aunt Mary.

"Shall we say this afternoon, father? It is a long time for little hearts to wait till to-morrow," was the answer.

How I remember it! The thrill of pleasure (which it was given to my Aunt Mary to stir) gushed through the veins, not really for that I should have the pony sooner—though that was much—but that

"— TO GOO MY GOOSES"

it was Aunt Mary's thought; a thought so like her: another instance of her own peculiar and distinctive grace to treasure up for ever.

Venturing once in other years when that young devotion had ripened, rather than changed, into the assured affection of privileged companionship — venturing then, though even then with but stammering speech, to give my Aunt Mary some insight into the depth of that child-love, I repeated to her in short what I have here at length detailed.

She told me it brought to her mind a little incident which had touched her a good deal at the time, though evidently she had been far from fathoming the deep-down spring from whence the momentary ebullition had gurgled up. It would appear from my aunt's telling, that that little fable of myself, the child in the frock and pinafore of four and a half, was one day endeavouring with fat inexperienced fingers to refit some little broken-off geese on to a toy stand, when she, as the good genius, came to its relief, and lighting a taper from the chimney-piece proceeded to fasten them on their pegs with sealing wax, the child, I, meanwhile standing by absorbed in the interest of watching the process. In the middle of it Aunt Bessy came into the room. With a hutch of the shoulders, and a flushing of face, and the clumsy jump of a rejoicing puppy, the little two-shoes exclaimed in extasy.

"Oh, Aunt Bessy! do you know Aunt Mary has lighted the candle *on purpose* to goo my gooses!" emphasizing with a crow of delight the "*on purpose.*"

I remember the toy perfectly: it was a flock of white geese on one of those movable stretchers which expand and contract on the scissors principle; but I have no recollection of the circumstance, yet it tells, after its child fashion, how early that chord was strung which has thrilled so frequently to the like touch even to latest years.

What is that power that reaches our soul, and wherein does its great strength lie? Not, I am bold to say, in the deed; but in the manner of it, a tone, a look, a way—just a way; what is there in these that they should stir and quicken the heart's spring? Unsubstantial and evanescent are they; but the spiritual is unsubstantial. "Le style c'est l'homme." What, in fact, are "those nameless graces which no methods teach" but emanations from the spirit itself. Nay, are they not the very spirit in expression?

In my Aunt Mary's case, I suppose, it was the gentleness of the womanly nature and the repose of the well governed mind; the combination of tenderness and strength on which it is so sweet to lean; aided by that choice gift of delicacy in perception which guides, as an instinct, to avoid the jar, and to discern the want, and to grace the kindness by the manner of doing it,—the home and familiar experience of all which has so often sent me away in the sweet exulting appreciation of the charm inexpressible, saying to myself, for lack of a better analysis, "It's just like Aunt Mary!"

But to return to the colloquy in the dining room and its results.

"If you please, Mary; if you please," settled the matter; and that afternoon, I, in the seventh heaven of sublimated happiness, walked by my Aunt Mary's side, and returned leading back the little bay pony which was henceforward to be, for three successive summer holiday times, no trifling ingredient in the overflowing cup of joy. The charm of it was inexpressibly enhanced by my Aunt Mary's arrangement that its pasture should be the lawn in front, and that a certain apple and lumber room, which opened out on the west lawn, should be cleared, and given up to me for a stable. Thus was the hardly credible happiness realized, that I could jump out of the west room window, fetch up the little creature, saddle it, groom it, or lead it about at all hours of the day at my own pleasure.

A word about the "West room." My brother Henry was at this time lame, and his pleasure was in joinering, and in other processes of ingenuity which make what is called "dirty work"; and this room was given to us for our unrestricted domain, to joiner, rummage, and have supper in. It was ours from this time forth in every holiday six-weeks, an Elysium of freedom and joyous happiness. From its window we shot at rabbits with cross-bow and pipe-stumps, and with bow and arrow; laid wait for birds; and scrambled in and out at our free pleasure.

Every day of this happy year was filled with enjoyment. The only trouble was how to get rid of the night which broke in upon it. There were the bathing excursions at high tides, and at other times longer rides than the donkeys had permitted before. There were the strawberry beds and the gooseberry bushes for interludes, evening walks round the wood with Aunt Mary, or merrily with Aunt Bessy over the Bronc to Margaret Lace; and here let me record how untiringly kind and watchful was Aunt Bessy over that poor woman, about whom there was a painful history of which I then knew nothing.

And there was at any time a ten minutes looking-in at the school with one aunt or another. Our aunts had in their very early days established a school with their father's encouragement; and he had caused a garden tool-house behind the south garden wall to be made fit for that object. It was afterwards more enlarged, and fitted with an oven to bake the children's dinners; and a small play-ground was added, fenced off with a rustic fence of woven willows. To my mind we may lose much by architecture and endowment. The large schoolhouse now conspicuous near the church, built and endowed by my Aunt Mary at the close of her life, according to her father's provision, will never equal in homely usefulness, and certainly will never have the charm of the garden shed and its willow-fenced play-ground.

Let me recall that garden-school before its memory dies with ourselves. Let me recall it with its little tenants in simplest cottage dress, and old Esther Brown the worthy mistress, herself a cottager, in " bed-gown " and " lindsey coat," untrained by government rule, but skilled in all rustic craft of the needle. Let me in imagination take the three or four minutes' walk to it from the North room, by the narrow door-way into the garden, through the swing gate,—ah, what magic in the sound of that gate, and the click of its iron fastening! Let me, even now, yet once more linger along the avenue where in spring-time the primroses clustered so bewitchingly in the grass by the tree-roots, and where in summer the shade was so cool; then pass on by the short narrow pathway, and the wooden door with rustic latch, into the little pleasant precincts, behind a garden, yet in a garden, for the gardens were various; and this, called after the pigeon-house which was at the end of it, was given up to careless cultivation of potatoes, gooseberry bushes, apples, Morella cherries, and to the pigeon's feeding table. To me it lost much of its charm afterwards by being converted into a straight-lined nursery ground with orderly rows of young trees and beds of seedlings.

The school so situated, "the ladies," by which term our aunts were designated, could any of them

THE BACKWAY FROM THE PIGEON HOUSE GARDEN.

THE LITTLE SCHOLARS

step over for five minutes in house attire, without difficulty; sheltered alike from sun or moderate shower, and hence it had the benefit of their daily frequent presence, a benefit not easy to calculate in its worth and extent.

Our aunts were gentlewomen by nature as well as by birth and up-bringing—the real china and the true gold which does not tarnish by wear. Refined rather than accomplished, their peculiarity lay more in the excellence of the grain than in the embellishments. Delicacy of feeling, gentleness, courteous kindness, were instinctive in them. They could not have framed their lips to a rough word; yet they spoke sound and homely sense. I think perhaps the charm of their manner in converse with the poor lay in the grave respectfulness of it, in the tone of fellowship which testified to their common nature.

The children, thus closely thrown in contact with goodness and refinement, could not fail to be in some measure inoculated with the same spirit; the frequent little messengers to the house for tape or needles, or the bottle of medicine for the sick mother, trotting the pleasant back way, through the stiles, by the pigeon-house and the pollard willows, no doubt looked upon its kitchen and servants' hall with somewhat of the awe and love with which its other rooms had inspired my own young years; and thus the bond of attachment and respect (I might well say reverence) was woven, only to be strengthened in after years; for the kindness never failed, and the tone of voice never changed: every cottage knew well the home sympathy of it, and each and all were familiar with the welcome presence; and thus is to be explained the grace of rustic gentility among the cottagers which then often struck strangers as peculiar to the place.

It must be remembered that then the Hall stood alone ; if we except the Parsonage, the sole stock of gentry in all the wide district of moss and sand-land. There were none to help in the care of the people, and none to divide their allegiance. This isolation, with its accompanying peculiarities, gave a character of its own to the place. It was a solitude, but no rude solitude. The college friend and visitor of my grandfather, who, on finding himself for the first time in sight of the solitary house, after his long rocking over the roads of sand, exclaimed " Why, Formby ! you have the heathen for your inheritance and the uttermost parts of the earth for your possession," would have rescinded the first charge on better acquaintance.

Yet there may have perhaps been too much of the clan exclusiveness in the hearts of these kindly people. I know not whether equal cordiality and honour would have been extended alike to their unallied betters. We must allow there existed an unreasoning antagonism against " foreigners," and this I will not pretend to justify.

But holiday time, like all things, must have an end ; and the day came to go.

We returned to Accrington, and were presently afterwards fixed at Clitheroe, for the sake of Mr. Allen's tutorship for my brother Henry. Clitheroe is the dreariest of all my remembrances. Cribbed, cabined, and confined in a small new unpainted lodging, in a down-hill row, at the fag-end of a country town, where it ever rained ; with a plot of building ground in front, walled in with cobble stones, and turned for use in the interim to a cabbage garden, it was a phase of life dull, dreary, and desponding. A not very distant field was used as a tan-yard ; and one could discern the outline of horses brought there to be killed. I looked over it upon Pendle's lion—couchant form—till I was weary of its shape; and I pondered meditatively over the strings of lime " galloways," as the author of "Scarsdale" seems likewise to have done before me.

This year was marked by some political events. George IV. died. I remember my father bringing the news to Formby, and speaking of it when I was loitering behind my betters under the old fir trees in the wood. I also remember my father reading of, and descanting upon the Paris revolutionary "Three Days," some few weeks afterwards under the dome at Accrington House.

I resented the dethronement of Charles X. with something of a personal feeling, as having so often seen him, and wearied myself in his palace gardens, and having moreover been once sent back by the Swiss guard, at the point of the bayonet, to have my hair put in better trim on his return from St. Cloud to the Tuileries.

" On n'entre pas en papillotes—Le Roi est ici."

This at the time suggested the imposing idea of a royal personal supervision from the infinite exaltation of the palace windows.

Christmas time has associations with Accrington House, as summer with Formby. We spent it there on this and other years.

Among the early Accrington recollections float the sound of church bells, alternating with the quick trot of horse hoofs down the carriage road, as the more modern family coach of this more modern grandparental home took a share of the party to church on Sunday mornings. The seat in the gallery looking down on the clergyman in his desk, and on the flaxen and red heads of the Sunday National School boys, whom their monitors kept flipping with a pocket handkerchief, or very audibly rapping with a wand ; the drowsy voice of the good pastor blending with the dying light of the winter evening ; the sudden upstarting, as of a multitude escaping, as the last words of the blessing died away, and the clatter of clogs and hustling of rejoicing children—with what clearness does all this re-live in sight and hearing, at times now, in the winter gloaming when rain and dimness show through the window frame as they did through the church window of that time, when, with a drowsy shiver and an effort, one left the stuffed pew corner which had grown warm, and went out into the wet churchyard, among the clattering clogs ; rain and dimness present, and the blaze of a large fire prospective, along with all the specialities and concomitants belonging to those rooms and their in-dwellers at Accrington House so well known after their kind ; but not directly belonging to the thread of this narrative.

And yet a word might not unfitly be given, if but by way of contrast, to the more Saxon characteristics of the maternal stock, and to the distinctive features of the East Lancashire population. The Saxon element of strength, the solid and massive in contrast to the refined and graceful ; the arithmetic and mathematics, as it were, rather than the poetry—this cast of character and habit has more of respectful appreciation, of interest, and of value, to my maturer judgment than it won then in those less comprehending younger days. The Accrington home did not harmonize in full with the early nature, spite of many pleasures and much kindness, and special merit and excellences more fully recognized at a later date. And yet remembrances of Accrington and its in-dwellers, of certain damp corners under dripping trees ; of the click of a certain door ; the very sound of a passing foot-fall under the dome ;

the character of a room; the figure of my grandfather Peel, powerful in mould, stern, silent, ascetic, commanding respect and deference; of my grandmother, easy, good-natured, shrewd and old-fashioned in speech, and all my own inward impressions connected and ingrained with these outward things—these remembrances are amongst the most vivid and the most frequent of those reproductions of the past which, often in these altered and distant days,

> ". . . As on my couch I lie,
> In solemn or in pensive mood,
> Will flash upon the inward eye
> Which is the bliss of solitude."

And to these impressions I owe not only much of reflective interest, but also much, I am well assured, of sterling good. The strength and reality of the Accrington nature—not unlike the character of the house itself, its outward solidity, its mahogany doors, its stone staircase and iron balustrade—has overlasted childish and girlish inaptitude, and stands out to mature judgment honorably recognized as that element of genuineness and truth in character and morals, so all indispensable as groundwork to whatever beauty and finish of superstructure nature or cultivation may raise upon it.

Manufacture and agriculture—stability and progress, (stability! some would say stagnation)—the silent solitude of the wide shore, and the hum and clatter of an operative village—these the characteristics of the two places, so different, are not more different than the tone and constitution of the two families of Accrington and Formby, with their several merits and demerits; or I will rather say peculiarities. And again,—how different in each case is the then to the now! How entirely has the present generation on both sides diverged, in its mode of thought and habits of life, from the last but one!

Reading the other day some of George the Third's correspondence with Lord North, I recognized in the good old king, whom it is the present fashion to decry, the tone and character of those I have known of his era—the royalty notwithstanding. In what this resemblance lies might not be easy to define. Possibly in what we should call its narrow-mindedness, its prejudice and positiveness as well as in some other more truly estimable points. No doubt the cast of thought *is* narrow-minded and prejudiced, according to our present lights; but viewed tenderly in the lesser ray of that dimmer era, far less conspicuously so—and, without venturing any plea for narrowness of views, I may at least be permitted to regret that, in rooting out some of the social errors belonging to our forefathers in more antiquated times, we should have rooted up so many of their graces also.

As the early weeks and months of 1831 glided into spring, I checked them off in secret reckoning, rejoicing with the more confidence as each in succession brought the summer period of Formby promise more within grasp. In that unlovely garden plot opposite our Clitheroe lodgings there was an elder-bush which spread over the wall. My room looked upon that plot; and as I sat there with my lesson books before me, each day I noted its buds and first leaves, measuring the time by it. When in full foliage the time would not be very distant, when in flower it would be close. The tree as it grew greener, grew my friend, and with its progress all other surroundings in that joy of anticipation, also grew more amiable in my eyes. In all future there is uncertainty; that was the one trembling drawback, and it was not till we were actually packed in the post-chaise that I could discard all dread of mischance and give the rein to rapture. I caught sight of my elder tree as we drove off from the door, and I pitied it, as I did everybody that stood in unjourneying guise on their own doorstep, unprivileged, and unblessed.

"Rose in Whittles"; that was the sign and title of a little inn at which we baited, as we had done aforetime on the like journey. I remember the sun broke out there upon the clipped yew-tree in its rustic garden during that happy but impatient hour.

But when we baited there on our return six weeks after, there was no sun-break. Ah! how different can the same place seem at different times! when joy is sparkling before us, and when joy is left behind! In looking back upon my life, I do not know that I can recall an hour in which just the mere sense of desolation and purposelessness pressed so heavily upon me as on the return to Clitheroe after this visit to Formby, which was, I think, the happiest of all the most happy of the child period. I was utterly heart-sick and objectless—mine was,

> "A grief without a pang, void, dark, and drear;
> A stifled, drowsy, unimpassioned grief
> That finds no natural outlet, no relief
> In word, or sigh, or tear."

And just merely to get out of sight I went listlessly up into my room, and sitting myself on the trestle bed kicked my feet about as they dangled down, while I passed over in my mind the dead level of cheerlessness before me. In this kicking process I kicked off a shoe, which falling, so to say, on its face, discharged a few grains of sand on the floor, the very actual sand that had been so dear from infancy! a very part of the place itself! O why had

I not thought to bring a pocket full that I might look upon it and touch it? I hasted to collect those few grains. While on my knees so doing, our landlady came in, warmly inclined, with words of welcome. Good woman! She little understood the facts of the case. To be glad to see one back here!—and from there!—there was something quite fiendish in the mockery of it. It was too rude a drop in the cup of disconsolation, and irresistibly it made it run over. I hated to cry: it was so girlish and contemptible; and I did my best to brave it out, but it would not do. Mrs. Brewer was embarrassed, and asked kindly if anything was the matter. The matter? there was matter enough! But what could she know about it? She that had never seen Formby, that was contented with Clitheroe, and with her house, and her senseless spotted dog that I had made the best of in the spring when hope shed brightness on all things as she danced laughingly before me; but now,—now, that I could not bear to think of. I made a choking unintelligible sort of excuse, and Mrs. Brewer retired, no doubt thinking I was in some disgrace that she had best silently leave to blow over.

Ashamed, irritated, I got up from the sand grains, and turning to the window, my eye was confronted with the elder tree. It was blackened and battered with some past storm. How it sank on my spirit! What did I care for its leaves now? I hated it, poor innocent helpless thing, it, and the garden, and the road, and the houses on the hill, and all the cold unsympathizing objects that seemed to mock me and my dislike to them by their impassiveness.

Does this seem all a "fantastic wantonness of woe"? I can but relate it as it was. I cannot debate about its reasonableness. It may be very childish, or very unchildish, to have cherished so intense a love for a tract of land ; but if I must tell my tale, I must even tell it unrestrictedly. And besides, it was not a tract of land only that so bound the heart, there was the human kindness, the element of moral beauty to sanctify the spell—more than all other, there was that deepest love, that heart worship given to her who, in child faith, embodied all perfection of goodness and wisdom ; and yet, in the midst of her great concerns, cared tenderly for my insignificance. And what better thing, I would ask, would you picture for this world or a higher ?

Ah ! in those young years, the very stay and beacon-light of my soul, and, in all after years, the dearest of all those who all were dear ! If love, the truest and purest that this earth can foster—love lasting and unchanged, can pay a holy debt of most blessed influence, that debt, deep as it was, has yet been discharged.

Was there anything fantastic or unreal in that love, or anything of selfishness or vanity ? My heart acquits itself of the charge. It was a love which, could I but now lay it, in all its fulness and unquestioning faith, as my soul's maturer offering at the Saviour's feet, would need no change.

But I have wandered into bye-ways and anticipated —and yet, perhaps indeed, it would be wisest not to retrace. Why should I weary my friends with repetitions ? Once to have told of the little bay pony and the West room may be enough. Those joys that at the time were superlative, and are, even now, how sweet in remembrance ! may be a wearisome tale to others. One may recur to things once too often. Yet there were some special features in this visit—the painters were in the house, and the drawing room was repapered; and looked marvellous in my eyes with its crowded pictures on the red flock. At that time our cousins Helen and Anne Formby, and yourself also at eight years old, were of the party for a fortnight—Lonsdale also for a few days. At that time we built a bower in the wood, and lined it with green boughs and moss, and held a feast in it, and at that visit one rainy day when our Aunt Bessy was playing and singing to us in the North room, my grandfather, attracted by the music, looked in, and taking one of the "little folks" by the two hands, pironetted with her round the room, and so doing suddenly fell down, having broken the tendon of his heel called Achilles.

This circumstance created a revolution in the proceedings. The stroke of a thunder-bolt would not have more appalled my aunts. The consequences did not prove serious; but close confinement was necessary for some time, and it served to bring before me more evidently the devoted filial love that watched with a lynx-like intentness for every means of offering interest and relief; a watchfulness which might, I can conceive, have become fussy and tiresome if it had not been of so reverential a nature.

I am reminded here to notice what was to me a pleasant evening amusement when I was admitted to it, viz., the clearing from gnats of my grandfather's bedroom. Gnats were a feature of the place. Possibly anywhere else, so abounding, they might have been allowed to be disagreeable; and such indeed was my grandfather's opinion of them, as one would occasionally disturb his slumbers with its persistent investigating hum.

My aunts, and uncles too, when any were in the old home, and such other guests as had attained to the discreeter years of late dining, spent the rest of the evening with my grandfather in the dining room.

Generally after tea my aunts read aloud; politics,

family and business matters, and generalities were discussed; and altogether it was a phase of being very august, but overpassing the limit of juvenile ambition.

An hour or so before prayers dismissed the conclave, my Aunt Ann was wont to go up to my grandfather's bedroom, and, there sitting in the dusk before the window, to watch for and slay each gnat as it flew towards the light. To her it was a serious and even anxious work; but to me, when I was admitted, a very gleesome chase. My grandfather's bedroom was approached by two steps and a sort of little vestibule, and contained a small inner dressing-room whose window looked into it, an arrangement which appeared to me very distinguished. There was also in the atmosphere of this privileged chamber an impressive dignity at that evening hour—perhaps, had I enjoyed my present enlightened views, I might have adjudged it close. The room was to the south, over the dining room, and had the same single, thick-mullioned window, of long width, with the diamond panes; and its one narrow casement door being always closed early, to keep out all breath of damp air, the heat of the day's sunshine remained in the room. This weight of atmosphere combined with the very dark and heavy curtains, and the dim light, and the reverential bearing of my dear aunt, gave the room a sort of regal dignity in my youthful estimation, which yet could not repress the glee of the gnat hunt. I am not sure that my aunt in her heart quite liked the merriment. I could fancy now that it would seem to her unbefitting the honoured surroundings; but she was too kind to repress it; only she objected to my unsanctioned hands shaking the curtains, which was a process necessary to disturb the gnats. This she preferred to manage herself;

doing it with no careless, displacing hand, but deferentially, and without disturbing their order.

The devoted love that my aunts cherished towards their father was intensified to the fullest in our Aunt Ann's case. There was something almost painful in that intensity that never could be permitted its utterance in words.

For some time after his death she secluded herself, unable to bear the jar of life's common interests, nor could she hardly ever from that time venture a direct allusion to him. For long years after, the well-known phrase, "It was said," or, "It was always the custom of this house," was well understood by us all as a reverential substitute for the mention of our grandfather's name, and in that sense sometimes by us with youth's chartered impertinence quoted in private.

Long years after his death, and but a few before her own, I was surprised and deeply touched by my aunt's entering one day very fully into the subject with me. This happened during an unwonted excursion, in the two-wheeled carriage of my grandfather's invention, to pay a visit to his, and all the family's friends at Halsnead Park and Sandfield. My Aunt Ann there broke through her usual reserve, and described to me how she had treasured up a chance remark, a look of tenderness; how she had watched for that beloved father in a morning as he came from his room, (latterly at a late hour) that she might not miss the morning greeting; that she might, if nothing more, but only hear the pleasant tones of his voice in the mere ordinary address of "Good morning to you, Ann, good morning."

When I told her how well I remembered those tones, that voice and manner; and that I could then call him before me as he would look into the North room at luncheon time, and just say, "Well

THE CHARM OF MANNER

little folks!" When I repeated this in his own tone and manner, her heart warmed to me, and the tears flowed; and I am convinced that she loved me more from that hour than ever before.

During this little interlude she also told me that the two labouring men who, for their strength and size, were chosen to carry him up and down stairs during the confinement consequent on the rupture of the tendon, had said it was worth coming miles just to hear him say, "Thank you," as they set down the chair. I do not remember the exact form of speech of our good friends, as my aunt repeated it, but it was heartier and more effective than as I have put it.

I have myself a vivid remembrance of another little scene at that same period.

Tea having been for some reason ordered in the North room, I was commissioned to carry a cup to my grandfather in the dining room. Careful, as it became me, not to spill any of the tea in the saucer, I opened the door cautiously, and quietly advanced. The light was the lesser gleam of firelight, or of a shaded lamp. My grandfather sat by a side-table, talking to my father with his usual animated and earnest manner. He did not notice my entrance. My father, who I remember was very still and silent, signed to me to put the cup on the table, and to sit down on the footstool which was by my grandfather's side. I did so, and remained there some time, and listened to that wonderful flow of speech on subjects that were distant as the moon from the grasp of my comprehension. My grandfather always moved about a good deal in talking, using some amount of action. He several times moved the tea-cup from him without receiving its presence into his mind; but, in the course of action, his hand came in contact with my head, and thereupon awaking up to the facts of the case, he exclaimed, "Ah little mousie! little mousie! are you there, little mousie?" and with the courteous politeness that was his very nature he gently stroked down the head of the "little Hebe" who had brought him "the cup that cheers," and kissed "the hand that offered it," abandoning, while I waited to return with it, the subjects so beyond my level, and graciously enquiring into our West room doings.

I linger upon the memories of my grandfather, for there is a grace in them, and a grace in the time they belong to—a glamour and a witchery of fresh young impressions which belong to earliest youth alone,—to that time of ungrounded trust in the stability of all things, and of that presumptive right of ownership in them also, which childhood claims in all it loves.

As added years gave experience of difficulties, and complexities, and hard responsibilities in life's course that never clouded the child-imagination, they did but,—they could but, make one better understand the value of the unwavering principle of duty, and the rarity of the singular unselfishness which were the especial attributes of our aunts' characters. The love and the honour have never abated, the value has increased; but, inexorably, the peculiar charm of unquestioning faith, of unlimited trust in earthly infallibility has died out. That glory of sunshine, too, on the present path, and that sweet shimmering haze over the distance that it is given only to childhood's heart and eye to recognize—that peculiar sheen and glamour unavoidably faded with the simplicity, the irresponsibility, and the happy general ignorance, which is bliss unchided in childhood's years.

Therefore I linger over these last memories of my grandfather; for the boundary of this child era coincides with his death, which followed rather closely upon the holiday visit of the following year, and wrought the changes inseparable from such an event.

The cheerless autumn months dragged their slow length in the Clitheroe rains, diversified by some weeks at Harrogate, (but I loved not Harrogate), nor do its trim straight walks through the fields to the wells in the frosty early mornings, much lighten the retrospect. It is true there were the next summer's holidays to hope for, but this year had to be got rid of first; till then a next year can hardly belong to us. There was not the zest in checking off the weeks, that there would be when the turning point had been passed and one could say "this year"—that would be so different from the long-off doubtful sound of "next."

I do not remember how the change came about, but Christmas witnessed my farewell to Clitheroe. We spent it at Accrington, and afterwards proceeded to Lytham for a few months' stay, leaving my brother Henry domesticated with the Rev. J. T. Allen, as his private pupil. My brother Richard had been for some time at the Tonbridge Grammar School. Hence he is much less mixed up with my narrative.

THE GRANARY STEPS

Have I too ungratefully passed by all direct mention of the farm buildings, that large old block of weather-worn brick and flag-slate that comprised stables, shippons, barn, and hay loft, besides cart cover, and carpenter's working shed, and odds and ends of outworks, with railed-off croft for hay and straw stacks.

At the south gable end, under lock and key, was the granary. The steps up to it were on the outside, and underneath them was a den which served as a place to shut up dogs in, or as a calf pen, and also as an arena for the exhibition of heroism by taking perilous leaps from the top. The steps were of rough-hewn stone, altogether unprotected by rail, and being therefore considered somewhat dangerous, were naturally all the more attractive. The granary itself was very attractive, and smelt delightfully of mice; and, to say nothing of eating handfuls of wheat, the heap of wheat itself was very delightful to scramble up, and to sink ankle deep into, and to slide down from; and there were all sorts of farming implements there too, which enhanced the general interest and importance.

But these same granary steps have also other different associations: they were the scene of the first sorrowful parting of my life; and alongside of them I first understood how joy, melting out of the heart, may melt away also from all surrounding objects.

Towards the close of one of the earlier visits to Formby, a messenger came from my uncle, Dr. Formby, with news that suddenly summoned my Aunt Mary to his house on a not uncommon family event.

She had to set off immediately, across the moss in order to catch the canal boat at Burscough Bridge. The carriage had started already; but to cut off its round of twenty minutes by the road my aunt walked direct across " the Green," and one or two fields beyond, to meet it at the nearest point.

Longing to be allowed to follow her, if only at a distance like a dog, I stood at the back gate which I knew she must pass through, thus putting myself in her way. She took me by the hand as far as the granary steps, and there telling me I had better go

DESOLATION

back, gave me a hasty kiss and hurried on; clearly with no understanding of the desolation she left behind.

I ventured no plea for further grace; but stood still, and there remained standing, watching motionless, with an increasing void at heart, her every receding step.

She wore a white dress after the fashion of that day: I can see it now; it was scanty of fold, and had one tolerably deep flounce at the bottom; I watched the last wave of it as it disappeared in the distance behind some stunted fir trees, and then the clouds seemed to close finally over all. There lay the granary steps, and there on one side was the spacious field they called "the Green," with its slight undulation which marked it from all others, and, by force of comparison, made it seem almost park-like; and there on the other side stood the wood, the beloved wood, with the narrow beaten pathway to it. These things were all the same as they had been yesterday; but what were they to me now? All the world seemed empty. I caught the glancing of the carriage roof turning an angle of the many-angled moss road in the long distance, and a swelling of heart brought irrepressible tears, to hide which I took refuge in the wood until I could re-appear with a face sufficiently hardened to escape all enquiry.

Nor only then has such collapse, in its measure, ensued. At times also when, seated on the foot-stool in a darkened corner of the North room, watching the countenance and manner, the swelling of heart finding silent relief in the slipping on and off of the shoe heel, a knock has come to the door, and a summons has carried Aunt Mary away; and then it has been as when the cloud of April has gathered over the sun, and the light has darkened, and the air chilled, and we have shivered and sighed, and risen up from a day dream and gone our way.

I have said much of the deep devotion of my aunts to their father; perhaps I have not given an adequate idea of his peculiar tenderness and courtesy to them, or of his warm love to all his family. The home affections were never more beautified by piety and the graces of good breeding. It is a sweet picture I could never tire to dwell upon, were I not fearful to weary with repetition.

As my personal recollections of my grandfather, very clear though they are, are yet confined within the limits of childish observation, I think it will not be amiss to add here a few extracts from letters of his written to his daughter Ann when at school, first as a child, in Cheshire, and, somewhat later, near London as a girl growing up. These extracts, taken from a treasured packet of yellow and well-worn large letter sheets, are the only relics of my grandfather that I have at my command.

No. 1 of the letters is addressed:—

> "Miss Formby,
> at Mrs. Whittaker's,
> Higher Knutsford,
> Cheshire."

I take from it these few lines:—

> *"Formby, Sept. 16th, 1799.*
> You will I am convinced be so fully aware of the necessity of availing yourself of the great advantages you now enjoy and of the heartfelt satisfaction which will arise from unremitted endeavours to please those kind friends who have been so good as to undertake the office of instructing you, that advice even on this most important subject would be wholly superfluous.
>
> Be assured of our most ardent affection."

The following is written on the birth of his tenth and last child who did not survive many weeks:—

"*Liverpool, August 25th,* 1800.

Though I have now ten children yet every addition to my family is an accession to my happiness, for not one of you has hitherto been guilty of a single action which has caused me real anxiety. I trust that you will all continue good and dutiful, and as firmly attached to your mama and me, and to each other, as you have hitherto been; then God will bless you, and we shall be a happy family, which is perhaps the most interesting of all objects upon earth."

The birth of his last child was followed in two or three months by the death of its mother.

I add here a letter from Mr. Hodgson, the curate of Formby, preserved in the same packet, which will throw light on the character of our unknown grandmother, of whom my aunt cherished a somewhat indistinct memory with the deep filial reverence which was natural to her—indistinct probably from having been chiefly at school the two or three years preceding her death.

"*Formby, Nov. 28th,* 1800.

DEAR MISS FORMBY,

You will be so good to present my sincere thanks to your papa for a present, I yesterday received from Mr. Holme; a present which will ever be esteemed amongst the most valuable I possibly can receive.

The memory of your much-lamented dear mama, can never be effaced from my mind. Never did I know a person leave this world so truly respected, or so sincerely regretted by all her friends without exception. To be ranked amongst the number is to me, dear Miss Formby, a gratification not to be expressed.

Heaven grant that I may prove myself worthy of such a favour, by performing the duty I owe to your family.

I cannot help adding, that the dutiful attention which, I observe, you constantly pay to your good papa, will not fail to procure you the blessing of heaven, and much love and respect amongst your friends. By following his example and directions, you will, I foresee, tread in the steps of that pattern of perfection which, alas! you have so early lost.

May every blessing this uncertain life can give, be constantly poured upon your kind papa, yourself, and the whole family, is the sincere prayer of your
Very affectionate friend,
JACOB HODGSON."

Addressed to—

"Miss Formby,
   Trinity Place,
     Liverpool."

The following are again from her father. This is addressed—

"Miss Formby,
  at Edward King's, Esq.,
    Lincoln Inns Fields,
      London."

and bears the date—

"*Liverpool, Jan. 8th,* 1802.

I still promise myself the great happiness of seeing you towards the end of the first week in February; but my stay with you must be short, as I must return home to superintend the work-people who will probably have at that time begun to build a house for me in Folly Lane. I must confess that I am in part induced to build from the wish to have rooms in which the friends of my young folks may be accommodated and entertained in a comfortable manner. You are all of you without any exception so good and dutiful that I cannot do too much to promote your happiness."

and, on the same subject,—

"*Liverpool, May 27th,* 1802.

I hope you approved of the elevation of my new house. It will be a comfortable one, yet it is the desire of being as useful as possible to my children which alone causes me to prefer any house, however commodious, to my dear native place. Hereafter I hope we shall pass many happy days *there* together—the next vacation we shall not be able I fear to pass more than one, or at most two nights there, though I will spare as much time as can be stolen from numerous engagements for the purpose."

The house alluded to was one my grandfather built at Everton, near Liverpool, and there he chiefly lived while the education of his family was in progress. He had also a living in Somersetshire —West Monkton—where he resided occasionally. It was later in life that he retired permanently to Formby, there, " in his dear native place," living in almost entire seclusion to the end of his days, taking delight in his children, and grandchildren, and his own people, but seeing few of his many early friends.

The following also occurs in the same series of letters, bearing the date of—

"*June 24th*, 1806.

..... Your brother Henry[*] is highly delighted with the thoughts of going to Formby on Monday. I hope that he and all of you will always retain your love for my favourite home."

The hope here expressed was abundantly realized. The affection of every member of the family towards that dear home of their fathers was indeed singularly strong and deep. Singularly strongly, too, has it descended to their children, to one of whom, myself, it has been a heart sanctuary through all life.

This home love—this especial sand attachment shall I call it ?—is no doubt a natural inheritance ; for I can well believe it was in the heart of another Richard Formby long ago, in dictating that clause in the marriage indenture dated " 2nd Oct., 9th Chas. I. (1634) between Bridget Stanley, of Aughton,[†] and Richard Formby, of Formby, on behalf of his son and her daughter,"

" The said Richard Formby . . . agrees to settle his manor " and his chapel of Formby on his son, and, if failure of issue, " to his 2nd son, and so on, and in such manner, that the " same may remain and continue in the name and blood of " the said Richard Formby during the will and pleasure of " Almighty God."

[*] My father, Henry Grenehalgh Formby, the second son.

[†] Widow of Edward Stanley, third son of Sir W. Stanley, of Hooton.

In confirmation or vindication of what I have described, the following is copied verbatim et literatim from a paper sent to my cousin, A. L. F., by Jane Rimmer of the Bronc. The original is written on a large rough sheet of paper in which I had folded a trifling present sent to her in remembrance of days gone by. I have many a time in those days accompanied one or other of my aunts to see the dear old grandmother she alludes to, who, crippled by rheumatism, was wont to sit year by year in an armchair by the fireside. I see it all,—old age venerable and well cared for, "the nicely sanded floor, the varnished clock," the open door, the garden, the black currant bushes, the free stretch of sand-hill beyond, and the fresh wind blowing.

JANE RIMMER'S REMINISCENCES

March, 1868. [Exact copy.]

"When lying on this bed of affliction and sufferings my mind often wanders Back into the Past and to the Days of my Childhud when a Scholor in the day and Sunday School and to the Dear Friends who I used to meet there as well as to those whom I left at Home at that time who ware some of them sufferers and add need of my assestance tho only a child no Dought you will recolect my Dear Grandfather J. N. who was so very kind to us all and to Dear Grandmother in her helpless state, he used to help us on Winter evenings with our Mans Cathesism and schripture tasks for the Dear Missises F. Sunday School where it was our grate Privilage to attend with I shold think with 50 or more others and where I met meny Praps for the first time I was to associate with in after life; Some much older then my self who are now old womon now them selfs grandmothers, and others who are gone to there rest some of them your Dear Aunts ad the Pleasure of visiting them on there Deathbeds and Chering them on in there suffering by there sweet voices and everrary assistance at all times and in every trouble and they ware looked upon as one of there own Family—If they continued to behave in a Proper maner and to retain there modesty in single Life or creadable marages—meny of these gairls ware the Daughters of Cotaagers or and small Farmers and not not

A COTTAGER'S MEMORIES (CONTINUED)

a few of them Dressd by these kind Ladyes or there honoured Aged Father whose name is honored by every one who knew him; I well remember the Blue Duffel and Gray Frize Cloaks so kindly Provided by these Three Dear Ladyes and also the Cullerd silk Bonnets or Stuff maid from Dresses Belonging to them—I well remember my self and sisters Having each a Plade Cloak and straw bonnet which was much worn at that time But which I then considered to be very far inferior to those worn by most of the other scholars I well remember Easter Sunday when so meney of the guirls maid there aparence in these New Bonnets maid by Isabela Rimmer of Ainsdale where the Webs of Cloths ware cot out and maid at that time when I think of the small school in the Pigon House Garden and of these Three Dear Ladyes Coming in and so meny hapy Faces meeting each other every Sabeth Day in that neat lovely Place and the Sunday Morning when there youngest Brother Brought Home his Wife and she came to Pay a short visit to the Sunday school I well remember with Proud satisfaction I used to Pas throw the garden and to enter the Hall by the garden Door Into the white Hall* as that was always considered a especil favour for to be admeted inside by the White Hall which hapened sometimes on very Pirticuler ocacions some times with one of the Ladyes to receive a Presant of a New Book or with one of the other girls who was not well to get some refreshment I remember well the click of the small gate and the Butifull Cheries in the Pigon House garden Hanging on the Wail as If only yesterday and that Light-futted old Gentleman we sometimes meet on our way to the Hall whose light foot and silvery are with sweet smiling face bid us welcome and I remember him with his yongest Daughter walking as nimble as most yong men each Sunday Morning entering Churh by the Frunt Door From there carage and also Riding the white Poney in the afternoon I also well remember the Plesant times when all the yonge Grandchildren used to come and spene there holydayes at the Hall what a Busy hapy time it always apeared.

What I have mentioned of the Dear Departed Family of your very Dear and much Beloved Grandfather the Rev. R. Formby, Esq., of Formby Hall for meny years the Beloved Pastor and faithful Minister of Jesus Christ in Formby his native Place very near the Old Bronk House whear I was Bourn and mostly Brought up almost I masay under the

* The garden entrance was called the White Hall from its white flagged floor.

eyes of these Dear Laydes all I have sed I think I remember Before I was 13 year old for the Dear old Gentleman dyed when I was In my 16th year at the very time of my comfirmation I will remember the very solom time; I had for some years Previous to his Death been sent to the Hall with a small Present the first Birds of the kind wich Dotrals my late Dear Granfather shot each returning spring as he alwayes maid It a Point to send them as a Presant to the Hall and the old gentleman also sent as a Presant a Brace of the First Paterages he shot each season Boath of them Being good shots and each respecting each other tho not eaquel in Rank I also Remember very well the last Illnes of all the Dear Departed first your Grandfather I think in Sept. '32 then I Remember Being sent to the Hall almost Daly to Inquier How he was But alas the summons ad Been sent forth. The shepard truly was taken and the Lambs was left The Wole Vilage was in sorrow But his own Family was almost heart broken but God was with them and truly he bound up the harts of those sorrowing Daughters though It was longe they greved for there Lost Father yet thers was a Godly sorrow they knew that he would be found again and that they would go to him though he would not return to them."

One more tribute from another source of somewhat later date may be allowed :—

"I remember your Aunts; I cherish there memory, in fact I love and reverence there name. They taught me how to live, and how to die. They taught proper, sound doctrine with that kind loving tact that made you drink every word into your soul, never to be forgotten. I love the dear old spot, and all its old associations."

LETTER IV

February 19*th*, 1867.

My Dear Ann,

In my last letter, or chapter, occurs a passing mention of Lytham. Perhaps a place so connected with so many of our mutual interests, calls for the respect of an episodical notice.

This was not the first time I had seen it; my eighth birthday had been passed there with sundry memories not worth now recurring to. The ground of our connection with the place was my grandfather Peel's habit of there passing the winter, for the sake of a better climate than that of Accrington. For twenty years or more he, with one daughter or more, was regularly the tenant of that same cottage we have both since known so much of. Each weekday he took his regular walk on the green beach; a venerable figure, powerful in mould, and austere in countenance, with slow step, leaning on the arm of his more diminutive valet, (a decent man with bow legs, taken from the duties of under-gardener to fill that office); and each Sunday, one of the two sole bathing-machines the place was endowed with, carried him, and one or two elderly friends taken up on the way, to the then small white-washed church in the fields. I have a strong recollection of the comical effect of being conveyed one knew not whether forward or backward, and suddenly finding on the opening of the door that everything was in a different direction to what one had surmised. I confine the word "comical" to that puzzle, for there was nothing comical at any time in any thing that concerned my grandfather himself. How strangely opposite were these my two forefathers. The silence of the one impressed me with as much awe as the flow of high converse in the other. The gravity and severity of aspect of my grandfather Peel, though mellowed a good deal by the venerableness of age, were a strong contrast to the grace and courtesy of the Formby ancestor. Indeed the Equator and the Pole could hardly be more diverse than they were. Unfortunately I never attained sense enough fully to overcome the childish fear of my grandfather Peel; yet he never shewed any harshness towards me, on the contrary he always tolerated me kindly, though in silence; and even promoted me to some acts of honour in his service.

The year 1832 with all its coincidental memories of reform agitation thus found us at Lytham; and the society of Dr. Norris and his family forwarded us well into the spring, when both they and our Accrington relatives departed.

Meanwhile time had sped; the months had passed on towards the holiday visit; it was now but six weeks off, now but a month, now but a fortnight, and now the time might be reckoned by days. I longed for the Saturday night that I might tell to myself the intoxicating truth, that there was but one more whole week to get over. The anxiety for each morning kept me awake at night, and when the morning came the day seemed interminable to look to. Even the thought that another hour was past made my heart leap. Let me dwell once more upon this happy fever; it was the last time of such excess. As I have before said the child era closed with this year. Change was in store. When I saw Formby the next time after this last of the holiday visits, life wore another aspect; the stability of the long-known was a dream from which I had awakened. Hitherto there had been no change, no break in the family circle since I had taken my part in it. From this time it was as though the foundations were shaken; and one after another left a vacant place as year succeeded to year. How complete is this change now! the scene itself and its circumstances, all, how different!

> ". . . . The race of yore,
> That danced our infancy upon their knee,
> How are they blotted from the things that be!"

On this occasion, however, I once more reached the place in that confident security of awaiting happiness which belongs to the heart of childhood only. When anyone catches back for a moment the mind of his youth, it is not, I think, so much its hopefulness as its security that stands so forcibly in contrast to the mind of later years. Instability, disappointment, transitoriness, change,—these are the images that rise up familiar to the eye of experience. All things come to an end. "Vanity of vanities!" is the mournful refrain of the retrospective elegy. With childhood it is security, ease, confidence, "O king live for ever!"

As my memory runs over all the tract of youthful joys I do not know that I can recall any consciousness of more deep delight than that of awakening the first morning, after each arrival, to find the yesterday's happiness no dream, but to see its assurance in each familiar object in the loved room; of getting up to look out of the window upon the garden lying in the bright sunshine, with the dark mass of trees beyond its wall; and there standing, to look upon, to feel, to recognize the actual living possession —then hurrying to dress, so as to run out alone, and step the step of reality on the sunny sand of the garden walk, then on the darker soil under the avenue's dear shade, and there to yield an unworded thanksgiving in that silent consciousness of deep happiness, that "sober certainty of waking bliss," which I have felt, and to myself have in all calm truth acknowledged, there, how truly! how often! —and, in that fulness there only.

Here I call to remembrance an earlier record, made long ago when the pen ran on more freely, and dared even to stray into the mazes of measure and rhyme. I give it a place here to prove how ever-abiding and the same, has been the love that has bound me to this one spot of earth, this land of dear memories.

> " I do remember well the happiest days
>   Of all the happy course of childish ways,
>   Days that stand out apart from other times,
>   Days of fresh summer feelings, holydays,
>   Long, joyous, sunny, past in pleasant scenes
>   Of country living—daisies, daffodils,
>   Hayfields and harvests, freshest fruits and flowers,
>   Lov'd animals and charm of farmyard joys,
>   And frank, kind greetings from old labouring men
>   And cheerful cottagers and sunburnt maids
>   With harvest rakes, or pail of milk, or charge
>   Of other rustic kind—these images
>   Crowd in a lov'd confusion to the heart,
>   And bring a sense of happy rural joy,
>   Real and yet unreal, true in the dream
>   Of happy childish faith; but all too pure
>   And sunny for this tainted suffering world.
>
>   Days, warm in such spring-light, love can recall,
>   Varied with hayfield sports, and fruitless chase
>   Of birds and rabbits, walks in sandy lanes

TWILIGHT FEELINGS

Or morning journeys to the far-stretch'd shore,
Vast, wild and lonely, there to gather shells,
To listen, when at rest, to the mock roar
Of the rough tide, that seem'd to dwell within.
And dear was the cool rest in noon-day heat,
After the happy toil, by fir-tree shades,
Listening to the unceasing song of birds,
And to the cawing rooks, whose home-born note
E'en now is so inwoven with those days
That like a spell it falls upon this heart;
It wakes yet fonder memories, too, than these,
Memories of trust and reverence deep and true,
And love that haply sheds o'er all its due.

And then, as evening closed the term of joy,
With what a very pleasure-wearied sense,
Throwing aside the faded wild flower wreath,
The white peeled linden wand, the unstrung bow,
The bonnet crush'd with tumbling in the hay,
And all the soil'd and hardworn garb of day,
Loitering, I oft would watch the darkening trees
Until the lightsome heart beat noiselessly,
And secret awe stole round its daylight joy,
Because the scene, so fondly lov'd, seem'd chang'd,
And yet was dearer still, I knew not why.
Ah, then, a child, unreasoning and unlearn'd,
Earth, sea and heaven, and day and night, they spoke
Unknowingly, in whispers to my soul,
That entered voicelessly within its depths;
They sang sweet hymns all through the summer night,
They touched a prayerful chord at twilight hours,
And stirr'd a joyous sense in sunny day.
  Is it the spirit of our mother earth
That leads us into quiet haunts at times,
When yet we marvel that our steps are stay'd,
And that the silence and sweet lonesomeness
Answer our want with soul companionship?
'Twas it that spoke in the calm hush of joy,
That caught me now and then like daylight sleep,
When I was fain to kiss the grass, the sand,
And give my heart's love to the summer haze,
Thinking it most belonged to that dear land
That filled my childhood's heart with such strange sense
Of happiness half-felt, half out of reach,
But all unreasoned of.

> Dear were the darkening meadows and the trees,
> And dear the breath of the light evening breeze
>   That made such pleasant, pleasant sighing,
>   As tho' 'twere twilight's spirits flying
>   To whisper every leaf to rest:
> So soft it lull'd e'en joy within my breast;
> But I knew nothing why such calm was dear,
> Nor why in stillness love should sink most deep,
> And, all unheeding threw myself to sleep
>   In free unthinking cheer,
> Eager to wake to morning joys again;
> Yet those still sultry nights were stamp'd e'en then
> In the heart's depths, and pictured there remain.
>
> The thought of those times brings tears to the eye,
> With a yearning regret and a mingling joy,
>   As the soul owns the spell of their mystery."

I have often alluded to sunshine in these memories, and not necessarily always in a figurative sense—sunshine is, in fact, a feature of the place. For one cause, there is actually more than in most parts of Lancashire. The two different ranges of distant hills draw off the clouds from the plain. Pendle, and the Longridge range bring down many a shower and drizzle over Clitheroe and the rushy fields about Accrington, when the sun is bright on the sands of the Formby level. On an unwooded plain one is also made more conscious of its brightness, and the Bronc, the moss, and all the fields surrounding the Hall were without even the shelter of a hedgerow; and, again, independent of all license of fancy, its radiance is really brighter. The yellow sand when dry is the very tint one would use in a colour drawing to designate a sun streak. And the contrast of its warm tint tells also with effect upon the blue of the sky. Hence, that young belief that at Formby the sun was brighter, and the sky more blue than elsewhere, was not altogether the fiction of enthusiasm. And the same facts may also explain why the shade

CLEANNESS OF THE SAND-SOIL

of the wood seemed deeper, more cool and refreshing than any other shade; the contrast from the heat and unshadowed brightness made it, in fact, very peculiarly grateful as well to the eye as to the sense of feeling.

There is also another feature of the place which may have had its share in that undefined pleasantness that others have owned to beside those that had a birthright in it—and that is its cleanliness. Wet sand does not make mud, there was absolutely no dirt. I remember it was always my pleasure on changing the outdoor shoes to empty the sand out of them on the carpet, and make mimic sand-hills. I cannot now suppose this amusement could have been satisfactory to the housemaid department; but it did not make any real dirt, and was never represented to me as an indecorum. I think there is more in this fact of cleanliness than we have perhaps realized. It is not necessarily childhood only that finds a charm in going freely over field or pathway without getting clogged with mud, and in being able to sit down without hesitation where the fancy prompts.

No doubt, also, that the unusual characteristics of the place added an interest: the solitude of it, yet the cheerfulness; the aroma of antiquated form and spirit pervading both its refinement and its rusticity, the sort of metamorphosis of life in the entire removal from the ordinary world routine of gossip, and fashion, of letters, and visits, and public news. All this, and the novelty of such isolation, with the ease and freedom of it, combined to make it a refreshing variety to the few whom kinship or friendship brought as temporary sojourners.

The life of most country places is much the same as that of other places only perhaps duller, or at least quieter. That at Formby was not at all the same; but, whether for better or for worse, was at least essentially different. Now, that distinctive difference is obliterated. Brick and slate rise in forms suburban; and now the sunlight can no longer have its peculiar glimmer over the unbroken level, nor the shore the charm of its untrodden solitude; nor can the stuffed birds in the entrance hall, and the quaint pictures in its dark corners, have now that seeming conscious air of unique existence and unrivalled presidency over all the surrounding width of calm subservient vacancy.

In these its altered days of noisy paved roads, of a rushing steaming railway, of a daily post, and many incomers, it would be impossible to resuscitate the old unique life; for these things commonize all places, and would bring an air of the general world into the midst of the Sahara.

To you my imaginary collateral descendant of the twentieth century, when the old Hall will possibly be a museum, or a debating club, or the lodge of a people's park on the outskirts of a populous marine resort,—to you, standing among plots of villa residences, surveying your heritage (if indeed you have not incorporated it in a company) I would offer a picture of what it was, in contrast to what it may probably have become.

Things must either have fallen by a happy fortuity into apposite places, or the John Formby who, more than a century ago, laid out the wood, and embellished the south front of the house, must have had a very nice perception of the fair and the fit to give so pleasant an effect, indeed I might say, in some sort, so impressive an effect, with so much simplicity of material.

That the said John Formby was in truth a man of a graceful and cultivated mind, the following extract from one of a collection of letters, preserved at Formby Hall, will sufficiently prove. He was the

DISTANT VIEW OF FORMBY HALL.

son of Richard and Mary Formby; was born 1721 and died 1776, leaving an only child, the Richard Formby of these " Reminiscences," our grandfather.

"*Formby, Friday 17th.**
(Sometime probably between 1750 and 1760.)

... If I live I shall have spirits to rally such reserve. Is not friendship, true friendship, unsuspitious? Are we not bound by gratitude as well as choice to the inheritance of the truest friendship?

I s$^{hd.}$ have sent B——'s letter if I had not made the mistake. I have others that do him credit—great credit, I am enabled to see how much more feelingly he pours out his heart than I do. I am sure his feelings are not stronger, and yet he tells them more naturally. His letters were—are, very (*precious*) his correspondence has amused many a pleasant hour—they now sooth me.

Can I ever forget how my heart withered within me at Lathom, the last place of the last interview. I see him now, sat with Mr. Antrobus at breakfast in the window. My heart is particularly disposed to reject all sorrowfull ideas. It resumed its own wonted cheerfulness by the thought that Providence would yet a little lend such a man to those who could not bear to lose him, to the numberless petitions of the interested in such a life. Vain and weak! Is a good man to be with-held from receiving the Crown of Glory, the Palm of the righteous, because we, fond mortals, think his being amongst us pleasant and usefull. Must he be torne with the thorns and briars of bad health and a laborious profession because we wish it and foolishly pray for it? I have known this excellent man through the days of boyish folly, the hours of youthfull vanity, the whole course of stedfast manhood. He has less to be wished undone, and has done more for the preparation for the reward he is now enjoying, than any or all the many men I have known, and I have known very many, in the most intimate state of unreserved friendship.

I think, I trust, I believe, it is good for us, this heart-rending tryal.
J. FORMBY."

Space, silence, and solitude are, no doubt, effective matter to work upon. There would be something

---

* There is no date of the year. The Friday as letter-writing day held good then as later; for most of the letters bear that day's date.

besides in the contrast of grace and shelter after the almost desolation of the surrounding tract, and in the refreshment of shade, after the unwonted approach of three miles of broad sand lanes, with their three or four parallel tracks of deep cart-ruts cutting through the light sod and sand-drifts; lanes, though brightened with many a patch of creeping wild flowerets, yet all unshaded by shrub or tree as you drew nearer to the Hall, and only divided from the level fields by a thick wall of sand sods called a "Cop," well run over with short grass and flowerets like the lane itself.

The seeming end of this wide line of approach, though not the real one, (for it turned off abruptly at a right angle) led to a field entered by a white gate, a gate of round bars, well proportioned, and of very good form and workmanship. Another and another of these gates brought you into the immediate precincts of the Hall itself, with its mass of wood and shade embracing it, and you passed from the fields into the shaded avenue, and heard for the first time the sound of the horses' trot on the only hard and the only dark coloured bit of road in the manor.

Refreshed by the cool shadow and the rustle of leaves, you reached the oriel doorway which stood in the full blaze of the noon-day sun, looking on to the stretch of untrimmed pastured lawn, which was cut off from the field beyond by a line of water the width of an ordinary moat.

The entrance avenue-road sent off a branch along the western side of the house, and passing on into the wood which lay further on to the back, sheltering it from the north. This avenue-walk was bordered with a broad line of grass under the trees, wherein grew, untutored, and with nature's grace, successively snow-drops and daffodils, primroses and cowslips, by the roots, or in clumps among the grass. Fancy decoration there was none, or artful arrangement to

FORMBY HALL, FROM THE ENTRANCE GATE.

THROUGH THE WOOD AND THE BRONC

conceal or bring forward; and trimness was wholly wanting. Wherein lay the charm it might be difficult to tell; unless in that very unstudied grace of non-pretention, and in the stillness and the seclusion; and perhaps in the contrast of cool green shade under which you walked with the sun-glare on the level field skirting it westward, on whose sand patches the rabbits had established a miniature warren.

A quiet stroll of ten minutes or more further on through the wood itself, and you might pass from its broad walk to a narrow pathway; and at the end of it, letting the small narrow door, that was hung aslant for the purpose, fall back with a bang, you found yourself on the dry sand-drift in the field, with the small pink and white convolvoluses, and the bright yellow cinque-foils, straggling under your feet; and there on the other side of the sandy way that led to Southport lay stretched out, westerly, the breezy level of the Bronc rabbit warren with its numerous little tenants scuttering about, or peering from their holes with depressed ears. Close, short, and crisp was the peculiar grass that covered it. The right botanical name I know not. It is not of the kind to fatten short-horns; but it sends up no ragged seed-stems. The greyish green surface, smooth as a Brussels carpet, harmonized with the breadth and calm of the free space, with the freshness of the summer sea breeze, with the wide blue canopy above, and with the bright yellow of the sand-hill boundary in the sheen of the sunlight. The two cottage homesteads with the thatched roofs, that broke the utter solitude, fell in well with the scene, and the ripple of the atmosphere played over its breadth and its stillness, and gave it cheer and life.

There was companionship in that free space, silent, soothing, and refreshing. You might lean leisurely on the rustic gate, and look over that quiet expanse and unwittingly receive its influence in a placid strain of thought stealing over the mind, and elevating it from the hurry or the common-place of daily life into a purer and serener atmosphere. You might go forth there at even-tide and find perhaps that the meditation of better things came more readily than in more favoured haunts of wood nymph or river god, where nature had scattered her beauty and luxuriance with a far more lavish hand.

Yes, certes, O my incredulous friend! I am quite awake to the coming objection. I am aware that there are different media through which the same object may be looked at with very different results. I do not need to be told that this broad plain of sunshine, this free glimmering space with its fresh winds, may be seen from another point of view, and by a discordant eye adjudged a mere unproductive tract, a waste of acreage; and the white battlemented house, also, as little better than a place of banishment from the interests of civilized life, the favourite exile of an eccentric taste.

Most true also, that all inanimate objects are endowed with their life from our own spirit; yet the varying scenes of nature have assuredly varying characteristics which act upon us with a distinctive impress; and among these, deny not to the cheerful solitude of the sunny level its own especial though modest place. I claim no more for it than a distinctive character of its own, a placid impulse favouring contemplative thought, a soothing seriousness, in no rivalship to the more stirring emotions which cultivated beauty or mountain majesty may awaken.*

* Since writing the above pages, I have, in looking into the "Natural History of Enthusiasm" come across the sentiment here extracted as justifying my own assertion:—"As the gay and multiform beauties of a broken surface teeming with vegetation, when

IMPRESSION OF A FRIEND

In support of my belief that the place generally had a right to such modest claim of peculiar effect, associated ever with its own peculiar moral charm, I am tempted here to transcribe the evidently pleased impression of one unprejudiced by connection of birth,— Mrs. Park, of Ince Hall, in Cheshire,— though this her letter, written after her first short visit, refers to a later period than I am now treating of—a period when death had made its further ravages, and my Aunt Mary was left the solitary tenant of the Hall.

"*Waterloo, 1st August*, 1848.

MY DEAREST KATE,
    I find Annie has told you I have really been at Formby; really seen your good Aunt; had her kind welcome, talked and felt as if she were an old friend, caught myself calling her 'Aunt'—yes, been taken to the railway in the curious little carriage, and experienced the zeal of Thomas, just such a Thomas as I should expect at Formby. Then I saw the wood and the nursery — the quiet nursery where 'the children never cry,' and I went to the school and saw the civil schoolmistress, 'If you please ma'am' every other word—primitive and good,—and your Cousin Dora sitting in the midst teaching. I went into the storeroom and saw all the jars, and into the kitchen, and all over, and admired the pictures. That is, I should think, a very good one of your Grandfather by Lonsdale; but there is a certain Mr. Chute,* or some such name, a friend of your great grandfather, who especially takes my fancy—he always planted a tree at his place when your ancestor put one in at Formby; I like that. We talked much," etc., etc.

seconded by favouring circumstances, generate the soul of poetry, so with similar aids, the habit of musing in pensive vacuity of thought is cherished by the aspect of boundless wastes . . . (to wearied minds) such scenes are not less grateful or less fascinating than are the most delicious landscapes to the frolic eye of youth."

* Thomas Lobb Chute, Esq., of "The Vine," Hampshire, born 1721, died 1799. He was cousin and successor of John Chute, Horace Walpole's great friend, so closely associated with him in all the planning and decorating of Strawberry Hill. Thomas Lobb Chute was godfather to my father. He is represented in a red waistcoat, and the picture is particularly pleasing in countenance.

(As regards the interest of the mutual tree-planting the extract from my great grandfather's letter will shew that strong friendships were natural to his character.)

In all this I have wandered very widely from my narrative, which broke off in the summer of 1832 when the heart, almost troubled with the depth of its happiness, once more welcomed the sight of those objects that had lain there, pictured, brooded over, longed for, cherished, re-appearing in dreams by night, and in day visions of solitary retrospection, and woven into every thought and hope of pleasure. Once more, in the presence of those flat sunny fields, of those battlemented walls and diamond-shaped windows, deep in the thick shade of the sheltering trees; once more reposing, basking under their spell of inexpressible witchery, the heart again recognized the accord and fitness of those dear outward objects with the inner graces that tenanted them, their undefinable harmony with the sweet cheerful voices, the smiling countenances, and the light of the calm eyes within, with the excellence of deed and purpose, the charm of mind and manner that formed the child's high model of undoubted perfection; not questioned of, not reasoned upon, but quietly received into the heart as the sunshine and the summer were.

It is a matter of surprise to me that the memory often recalls with the clearness of actual existence the impression of some uneventful moments and occasions, while the stronger sensations of great enjoyments, or the keener impressions of marked events have lost their distinctness. To my inward sense there returns like a pleasant perfume the very atmosphere of an occasional minute or two, both in this and earlier visits, while standing on the stairs' head, and there passively gazing, and realizing the full quiet satisfaction of spirit flowing from the loved surroundings.

Over the stairs, and out of reach of all ordinary brushes or hands, was a window with a bust on the ledge—to this day I have never had the curiosity to ask of whom. Naturally summer flies congregated on that ever-closed window, and there died in hundreds—I fear of such hunger and disappointed hope as flies may be capable of suffering—and lay scattered on the wide ledge about the bust. Those dead flies did in no sort decompose the ointment of my happiness; but on the contrary have a fragrant memory.

On the walls around were the pictures of our ancestral connections, dark and discoloured, in worm-eaten frames. I do not think high artistic merit could be claimed for any of them. A little dog ambitious to lick his master's fingers could, in favourable lights, be deciphered in one; a young boy emerging from an extensive drapery of cloak in another. They had all collectively a grave charm, quite apart from any complacency of succession, which had nothing to do with the mind of those years. But, beyond theirs, was the charm of the narrow door at the stairs' foot, from which we stepped at once upon the sand-walk of the dearest of gardens, and to the right of which the close adjoining window admitted some view of the flower and shrub department. On that window, being in full reach of the domestic duster, only a few daily flies lay straggling, and among them the usual complement of lightly poised long-legged gnats. The clock ticked audibly from its unseen vicinity—not in any respect an uncommon sort of clock in reality—but then endowed with the pervading spirit of peace and joy which filled the encircling atmosphere.

The very sensation of summer warmth and careless ease comes back to me now as I lean almost in reality on those rails at the stairs' head, and recall that silent heart melody of pure rejoicing which flowed on without a lurking murmur of dissonance.

Different again, and almost over-intense, was the inward emotion with which, in evening twilight, sitting conveniently in an obscure corner on one of the footstools, I have in silence watched my Aunt Mary as she sat by the North room window making the sleeve of a certain checked blue and white silk dress; her work-box on the window ledge, which, being deep, served for a table—a dark leather work-box, somewhat time-worn—the self-same work-box she would bear the child's fingers of old to arrange, or, in juster words, to disorder according to their notion of fitness. Ah, well, that may be a trifle; but it is at any rate an eminence of forbearing indulgence, as I reflect upon it now, utterly beyond any capacity of mine. The work-box had a little gilt ornament at the top—I see it now; and the calm figure, and the turn of the hand, and the countenance that no description can render, and I hear the tone of voice that made my heart thrill, and I hold that that soul satisfaction, that "sweetness without satiety," that depth of devotion, and that absorption of self-consciousness in the contemplation of its object, as experienced in those still moments on the footstool, form as fair an earthly type as I am able to conceive of what we are given here to understand of the soul's contentment in a higher sphere.

And among these week-day records let me mingle a Sunday memory, a passing recognition of the walk to church in the white frock of young years, across the dear fields of light hay and corn crops, and flowering potato ridges, through the narrowest of

FORMBY CHURCH.

stiles, purposely contrived to admit the human form with every combination of difficulty. In those days my grandfather would often canter to church on the grey pony; the peculiar carriage being left to the guests. The church was perhaps the most modern feature in the district. It had been transferred in comparatively late years from the original situation in the sand-hills near Formby Point, there leaving the old grave-stones to crumble in undisturbed solitude among the wild flowers and the star-grass.

Rural simplicity characterized everything about the transferred sanctuary, simplicity of material, of congregation, of ritual, and of psalmody. Pipe and tabret, or more unfiguratively, flute and fiddle, added a doubtful melody to voices selected rather on moral than musical grounds. The black bonnet, the clean "bedgown," and the best "linstey-coat," were a common Sunday dress both for matron and maiden, and the sober holyday attire of fathers and brothers betrayed the hand of the rural tailor.

In contrast to this rusticity (and the contrast had its charm), was the refined grace of my grandfather's venerable face and figure, and the tender courtesy of his always rather impassioned address from that high pulpit in the sheltering glass frame-work he had himself devised to exclude draughts, or the energy with which he joined in the responses from the family pew, his voice, which had a clear and sweet ring, being audible above the clerk's, who, I think, made a respectful point of waiting to follow after him.

That pew, square, or, to be minutely correct, oblong; cushioned and footstooled, lined with thick green baize, and reached by a private entrance through an ante room, was sanctified I am sure, by as much genuine devout worship, and as complete absence of pride of distinctiveness, as the most orthodoxly carved oaken bench of this ecclesiastically enlightened period; which of us that can recall the serious anxiety depicted on our Aunt Ann's countenance, and the quiet earnestness of all its regular occupants, could bear an expressed doubt of it? The pew was instinct with the grave repose of the Sunday spirit. Not austere, but solemn, earnest. The religious spirit pervaded it, and entered into its dim light and somewhat close atmosphere as of natural affinity. Why, the very round-headed brass nails, which were ranged in a close ornamental row on the strip of faded gilt leather that encircled the pew sides, have in them, to my memory, the very symbolism of devotional reality.

A certain external anomaly might have struck a stranger in the livery of the servants' pew. It was of an unusually light stone, with blue facings, a contrast certainly to the sober colouring of all besides, and throwing into rather strong prominence the rustic form and gait of coachman and footman who were native, and moved with the peculiar heave which the sand roads imparted to the labouring footstep, but even this must be ranked among the distinctive touches and peculiarities, which added a charm of originality and distinctiveness to all that was so distinctively dear to the eye and heart of one young observer at least among the lookers on.

It was to me in those days a rather senseless source of exultation to note the dark hair of the surrounding agricultural heads. As may be supposed it was always sedulously smoothed down on entering the sacred building, as is the wont of those accustomed to the rubbing down of horses. Inwardly, I contrasted it with the red and pale flaxen of the East Lancashire race at Accrington, and with much prejudice to the latter. I am induced to mention this difference as an ethnological fact for those whom it may interest. I can give no rational reason why I then attached superiority to the distinction. No doubt there is in the life of the out-door labourer more of nature's touch to bronze the complexion, and give vigour to the frame; and the pallid hue and stunted growth of the factory operatives are due in a great degree to their very different life and habits; but, independently of this, I imagine there is a difference of origin. The character itself is different. I think however the flaxen race have, of the two, the more forcible nature, and, as a study of Lancashire character, would afford the more marked originality.

How entirely I have wandered from the straight line of my narrative which I am half unwilling to resume, because it must carry me away from the period when all was unshaded perfection, and with that period I must take a lasting farewell of the generation that is wholly passed from us, and that does not live even in the memory of many that now fill its place. I have not been, I think, fully conscious, till, in recalling these younger memories, the fact forces itself upon me, how much of grace and interest my grandfather's presence shed over all the place in those years. When I think of recurring to it, when his paternal rule and benignant authority are there no longer, I become sensible that there will be a void, that it will have lost a gracious presence, which I see now was a spring and centre of happy influences, not adequately discerned by my immature understanding while it was in action. The shelter and stay of their father's presidency, and the freedom from charge of anxious responsibilities, also gave to my aunts' characters a happier flow. They were less grave, as less oppressed with the weight of a position in which they must not only act and judge for themselves, but be themselves the centre of influence to all around them. The more feminine graces perhaps flourished most luxuriantly in their father's lifetime. Did in fact a sterner air of duty in later days overcloud in some measure that atmosphere of grace and courtesy, so peculiarly characteristic of his presence? Perhaps in a slight degree it may have done so.

My grandfather shed a grace over all he did. I have heard it remarked that he found fault and gave advice with a charm of manner and phrase which made the counsel attractive, and the blame palatable. The extract that follows must go far indeed to prove that the impression of that charm which now seems to attend his voice and presence in all the younger memories, is not an endowment of my youthful imagination only.

EXTRACT FROM A LETTER FROM THE REV. J. B—— AFTER HAVING READ A MS. COPY OF THE EARLY "REMINISCENCES."

" . . . . Who that ever heard that grandfather's lively and fascinating conversation, could ever forget it? I hear it now, I see his every gesture just as the writer has described them. . . . Can you wonder that I, in particular, should have read these 'Reminiscences' with deepest feelings when I tell you (as you perhaps already know) that to your revered grandfather I owe everything I have? He took me by the hand when friends were few; he lost no opportunity of promoting my interest from the very first day I had the privilege of becoming acquainted with him; he treated me more like an equal than as one far below him in respect of family and worldly circumstances. He bore with all my short-comings and deficiencies; he advised me in all my difficulties, nay, I cannot possibly enumerate the various acts of kindness I received from him, for they formed one continued series from the time I first became his curate to the very day when it pleased God to take him to Himself."

Indeed I am well convinced that when any influence has taken deep hold of the mind, there must

THE REV. RICHARD FORMBY, L.L.B.

have existed the force of a real cause to give it birth. Yes, I believe that, in truth, much of the secret of that aroma, that roseate essence of fragrance which seems to me, as I write, to distinguish the early Formby memories from all other best, whether of more home or more foreign experience, is due, in fact, to the graceful dignity of that powdered head, the graceful courtesy of manner and demeanour, the graceful flow of polished phraseology in the abundant converse, the graceful character of the inner mind which embellished retirement and simplicity with the manners of a court, and made license impossible where there was yet unbounded liberty.

These earlier days were dear indeed at the time; their joys were no unconscious joys even as they passed, and sweet, ah, yes, sweet beyond all others, is the fragrance of their memory!

> " How oft, in lonely rooms, and 'mid the din
> Of towns and cities, I have owed to them
> In hours of weariness, sensations sweet,
> Felt in the blood, and felt along the heart;
> And passing even into my purer mind,
> With tranquil restoration."

P.S.—I am sensible of an omission in the record of pristine peculiarities. I have not hitherto alluded to the absence of a post. In the postal world the place was not recognized as existing. Letters were despatched and received once a week by private mail, *i.e.*, the market cart; being despatched by it on the Friday evening, and received by its return on the Saturday; and this was not only tolerated, I fear I must admit it was viewed with partiality, along with the sandy roads that were the chief cause.

I fear truth compels me to confess that a regular post, and ·paved roads were, when glanced at as possible future contingencies, spoken of with that tone of indefinite alarm that free trade, and railways, and other startling innovations have sometimes evoked even under the diffused enlightenment of more advanced later days.

For myself, I have no objection to make a full and humble confession of my own insensibility to the modern advantages which will presently have re-civilized, perhaps rather reconstituted a spot of earth once unique in its gentle rural refinement and simplicity.

But then, I do not live there, and not reaping the benefit of suburban conveniences and suburban entertainments, I naturally am more impressed with the sense of a loss—the loss of an existing mundane sanctuary whither one might retire for the refreshment of freedom from the every-day and the common-place, and for the communion with an almost sacred past,—than with a sense of gain—surely a questionable gain; surely, at least, a mixed and qualified gain—in that the manners and tone of a commercial mart, its wealth, its speculations, its demoralizations, as well as its enlightenments, will soon have completed a war of extermination on the simple domesticities of what once was our own little private world among the rabbits and the sand-flowers; the home too of a quiet affectionate race of cottagers, whose little garden strips so bright with lilies and cabbage roses, fenced in from the grassy sand-lanes with white-washed palings, may have to give way to the dreary row, even and slated, and numbered up from one to one or more dozens; the unindividualized dwellings of "operatives." And where then will be the kindly interchange of benevolence and attachment, of influence and service, of tender care, and respectful devotion, which binds class to class better than treatises and declamations? There may be an in-flowing of knowledge, a rooting out of prejudice, an enlargement of view; but where will be the gentle charities? oh, where will be the homelike affectionate intercourse of the olden time, with all its softening and refining influences, softening and refining alike to the hall and the cottage?

But I bow, submissive, before the irresistible law of mutation be it towards progress or decadence. Well know I it is vain to resist the tide of change, and unwise to meet it with bitterness. Out of the new system may spring a new order of good. May it be so! I love the place too well not to wish it in all sincerity. Only suffer me, individually, to sigh for that in the past which can never be restored, since to me, individually, the future can bring no compensation.

"A TRUE DELINEATION OF THE SMALLEST MAN AND THE SCENE OF HIS PILGRIMAGE THROUGH LIFE IS CAPABLE OF INTERESTING THE GREATEST MAN."—*Carlyle.*

PART II

CHAPTER I

> " Behold the child,
> Happy in shelter'd vale, he plucks the flowers;
> But seasons roll—he mounts the rising hill,
> And widening prospects open on his view,
> River, and wood, and plain, the distant town,
> And, now, the far-off sea, ...
> . . . . While over all
> Arches the silent Heaven."

March 26th, 1867.

During a break of some weeks, my mind, recurring to these interrupted records, has been visited at times with the thought that in this oasis-like seclusion of the Formby life, rustic and manorial, there lies both originality and moral excellence enough to supply material for a peculiar class of romance, contemplative and reflective, dealing more with nature and character than with plot and events, —a class which meets with acceptance from minds by no means lowest in literary taste and refinement.

But successfully to construct such a class of romance demands the hand of a master—not so much of a master of fiction as of the subtler beauty of reality idealized. But I deal with Reality only. The mere vision, however, of such an ideal, floating only in the opal blue of imagination, all airy and unsubstantial as it is, has made me impatient and irritated with my own infantile records. And seeing they have arrived now at a fit concluding point, the further question arises, "Shall I pursue this record at all?" I ask this question of myself only. I involve no one in the responsibility of encouragement. Shall I, building on the worth of faithful representation of scene and character, proceed, and step forward into, necessarily, a more diversified field of narration? In answer, an inward impulse impels me onward to fill up the picture from the stand-point of more matured observation and judgment.

I pass on, therefore, to another era not only in my own but in the family history also, and close the period of the holiday visits, and of the child delights, with that of my grandfather Formby's life.

The last six weeks of the last chapter were the last of the little bay pony, the last even of the grey, for it was never again used after my grandfather's death, the last of the old régime—the last, also, of my aunts' more easy irresponsible life.

My grandfather had seemed to be as usual on our arrival, but gradually sickened during our stay, and became so far ill that we removed at the holidays' end to Southport, to be within easy distance; my father remaining at Formby to take chief part in the sick-room attendance. Each of the few times he came over to see us it was with a graver aspect. In about a couple of months the end came.

My Uncle Hesketh had brought his family to Southport to be near likewise, and I remember listening to the comments naturally made by my mother and Aunt Hesketh as to the great change. For my part I sat down in an out-of-the-way sand-hill, and tried to realize that the white head and beautiful countenance, the gracious presence, the active graceful life, and the flowing converse, had passed away from the place for ever. The young cannot, I think, realize sickness and death when distant. I was vexed with myself that I did not feel overpowered with grief.

Hitherto my youth had emancipated me from any concern with the graver affairs of life, and I had known of nothing beyond the outer flow of ease and happiness in the chartered Formby home. Yet, in truth, even in it there was a share of the common lot of sorrow. Differences had arisen between my grandfather and his eldest son, one cause of which lay in that son's over confidence in rash speculations, which had resulted in difficulties and losses, causing great trouble and anxiety to his father, whose nature it was ever to feel acutely in all things; and, consequently on his account, and their brother's alike, occasioning great distress to my aunts.

The distrust thus awakened in my grandfather's mind led to intricate testamentary arrangements, the one of which, most concerning these memories, being the leaving to my aunts, besides their other portions, the Hall and its adjoining land for their lives, with warm expressions of confidence in them both as to the present and the future. To this will he appointed, as executors, his fourth son, the Rev. Miles Formby, and his daughter Mary. I have been told by my mother, who had full knowledge of that time, that the verbal and written expressions of love and confidence towards his daughters, and this strong proof of their reality, were overpowering to them all; but to my Aunt Ann especially. How they justified, through all after-life, his confidence in and high opinion of them is known to us all well. All three, but eminently the two eldest, devoted their lives to promote in every way the good of the people and the land, holding themselves to be stewards, not possessors, of their trust, and anxiously putting forward this view in converse whenever occasion permitted. So much did they shrink from any claim of ownership that they would not have any other name on the farming carts than " Formby Hall," though exposing themselves to a fine, which, however, from kindly respect, was never exacted.

Through all future years my Aunt Ann would never say farewell to her oldest brother within the house door. On all occasional visits that he paid them, she made some reason for a walk or ride, so as to accompany him a part of the way; and then, at a turn of the road, would make a hasty parting in a casual manner. She had once said to her sister Mary, " I shall never, while I live, see John go out of this door to leave, and myself stay within." Those who knew that dear relative's scrupulous delicacy, can well recognize her ownself in this little trait. Aunt Mary told it to me one blowing, snowy, winter day, when I asked her with amazement what spirit had possessed my Aunt Ann to set out with my Uncle John, in weather that she would not have sent the footboy out for other than an imperative necessity.

I remember that my Aunt Mary added that in the duties devolving on her as executrix, she had to resolve to pass through many painful points, as it were, with closed eyes.

My Uncle John, through his wife, who was a co-heiress, had property not far from Liverpool, where he for a time resided with his family; and it was from thence that he paid the occasional visits to his sisters at the old home. These visits, as shewing that he affectionately regarded those sisters without grudge or jealousy, were honourable to his own feelings, and gratifying to theirs; but, unavoidably,

THE REV. LONSDALE FORMBY

there was an element of constraint in them. Perhaps too much sedulousness on the sisters' part to pay extra consideration, and to avoid touching on any subject that might awake painful associations, obstructed the easy flow of converse and feeling, so free and affectionate in the case of all the other brothers.

But the anxiety of these meetings, if really anxiety prevailed, presently ceased; for eventually this much considered brother married a second time, and afterwards lived entirely abroad till his death.

It was the ruling desire and object of the sisters that the chief of the property, at least, should revert to the natural branch, and this object they steadily and unostentatiously pursued. Theirs was the self-devotion, theirs was the patience and self-denial, while, outwardly, nothing seemed more simple and natural than when their oldest brother's oldest son, the Rev. Lonsdale Formby, in due time, filled his grandfather's place as pastor to the simple rural flock that had consisted mostly of his own tenantry; and when, eventually, he filled it more fully, as it were a matter of course, as pastor-squire.

[Now, this March, 1897, it is familiar to us all how, through many years then to come, and now past (for still I deal with the bye-gone), he, the Rev. Lonsdale Formby, filled that place, looked up to with an old-world loyalty, as hereditary ruler, adviser, and friend, in all the common everyday, as well as in the deeper needs of his farm and cottage folk, who had known him, as belonging to them, from his youth—nor, indeed, by those only. In the year 1886 there appeared a magazine story in "The Leisure Hour," the scene of which is laid in Formby under the name and title of " Marshlands," in which he, "that fine old Christian," is almost enthusiastically brought forward as the "Mr. Marshlands, of Marshlands," conservatively disliking all innovations, developments and improvements, standing, all the while, pre-eminent in all kindnesses, liberalities, and administration of good, alike to his own people and to the flood of "new comers," whom, says the writer, "in theory he detests," but to whom "in practice, he is the best friend."*

The magazine story deals with shipwrecks, and runs chiefly in rustic lines; but, in passing, I take note that it oddly meets, in some sort, my floating vision of thirty years back, that in the oasis-life of the Formby seclusion there lay material out of which a romance might be woven.]

Returning now from an extended digression, once more to the long bye-gone, I must, with whatever, regret, bid a final farewell to the child-world and the child-nature—the primrose, and (to borrow Horace Walpole's happy phrase) the "lilac-tide" of life—

"My May
Has fallen into the sere and yellow leaf;"

and I turn to look back upon that sweet season of freshness with a tender partiality. Truly all seasons have their blessings, and some beauty of their own, but the bloom and radiance of the year fades with the lilac blossoms, and, assuredly, the lilac-tide of our youth's first prime returns no more; and thus

* It is some satisfaction to me to include this slight tribute to my relative, my friend from early years, as these pages pass through the press. The Rev. Lonsdale Formby died on June 19th of the last year (1896), and his son now fills his place, the pastorship excepted.

bidding it now farewell, I feel that "Farewell" is a word that makes me linger—

> "De la jeunesse, de la jeunesse,
> Un chant me revient toujours—
> Oh! que c'est loin! Oh! que c'est loin!
> Tout ce que fut autrefois."

The autumn mornings were sharp, I remember, and the sycamore leaves blackened and fell, and frosty dew glittered on the points of the starr-grass, and I felt the chill mentally as well as bodily, while we yet stayed on from week to week at Southport. With the change at Formby a change had come over the spirit of my dream, and the anchorage of my life's hopes and objects was loosened. Moreover I heard hints about growing up, whispers of accomplishments, of manners and address, of masters, and of this and that hitherto permitted delight being now unseemly. It was a time of transition; and apprehensions concerning required elegancies and proficiencies, which, dimly understood, loomed threateningly in the indistinctness of the future, disturbed my careless peace.

The autumn sharpness had merged into the first fogs and frosts of early winter before we finally left Southport, then about as different from what it is now as are, now, most other places familiar to me in earlier years. Our cottage was a little nest (and so called) in a sandy dell shaded by a few battered sycamores, beyond the outskirts of the village, then a long straggling street of detached plain lodging houses at the back of the sand-hills, the paved strip of road between them being flanked with sand-drifts, and the houses having all bare plots of burnt up grass in front. The place boasted an apothecary's shop, a draper's, the usual amount of small provision depôts of one sort or another, one or two small inns or public houses, and an excess of donkeys, which, or rather the more unamenable drivers of them, gave the place an unpolished rubbishy seeming. As a bold innovation and invasion on the rights of seclusion, it was by the authorities at Formby viewed with prejudice and disrelish, and the extra difficulties of the road, or, more properly, sand-hill track, to it, were beheld with favour as a barrier to ordinary communication. My grandfather, and my aunts after him, would any time more willingly have sent a messenger fifteen miles in the opposite direction, to Liverpool, than the five to Southport. Yet we did occasionally make a riding excursion into the proscribed district, in consideration to youthful weakness that leaned towards novelties.

However the place may have amused or attracted as an object for an unwonted excursion, it had no favour in my eyes as a dwelling place: its sunshine was very ordinary sunshine, its winds were boisterous and dusty, its sand was common sand, and blew about blinding the eyes. I was glad to go. Formby would be further away, that was true; but, alas, it was already further, strangely further; for there now intervened between me and it, a feeling of awe and diffidence, rising up like a chill vapour out of the unfamiliar cloud of mourning that had fallen upon it. Shy and restrained in the presence of grief, inapt to comfort, unprivileged to offer sympathy, a consciousness of disqualification and exclusion presses on the young, and stands as a barrier between them and the bereaved, like the pillar of cloud troubling the Egyptians.

Our first move was to Accrington for the Christmas; and it was there, or had been before, arranged that my father and mother should spend the remaining winter months at Formby, as some stay to my aunts in their first bereavement, while I should be transmitted to the keeping of my grandfather and

Aunt Jane Peel at Lytham, it being considered that my age, or rather youth, made me an unsuitable adjunct at this time of solemn and deep sorrow.

My brothers joined us at Accrington from their different places of study. The Hyndburn and Church-Bank off-shoots at that time supplied no small addition to the family gathering at Christmas-tide.

The Accrington House life flowed on in its wonted way. The pool of quadrille, interrupted by prayers; the supper at nine with the question of toasted cheese, the occasional barrel of oysters, and the Saturday cockles and mussels; the scrape of the opening front door announcing the dropping-in of a relative; the stuffed peacock airing itself before the stove grating; the silent organ that nobody now played; the resounding of the foot-fall under the dome; the hazardous experiments made, child-like, in the ascent and descent of the marble-like stone staircase, gracefully winding with so many and so low steps, that were widely broad by the circular wall, and perilously narrow by the strong, but elegant iron balustrade; all the familiar rooms; the Waverley novels; the winding of the hanks of my grandmother's knitting yarn, and the mending of her musical boxes—my oft recurring occupation. These things were as I had ever known them : by turns they pleased and wearied me, but now, caught sight of in the long retrospective avenue, they are winged, and flit through the distant shades re-robed in a drapery of interest, which, at that time, they had not gathered around them.

In due time I found myself at Lytham. How I got there I have no defined recollection, no doubt by the usual means, namely, driving the whole long way, stopping only for an hour in Preston to bait the horses.

The Lytham life claims some record.

It was my grandfather's habit to rise early : about five, I believe. The family prayers were at half-past seven, punctual to the moment. Old Millicent tinkled the bell that summoned us downstairs. I have reason to know it, for I officiated. Lateness was out of the question—no one was ever late where my grandfather was concerned. A little before eight Millicent's voice proclaimed regularly in a melancholy cadence from the foot of the stairs, " Plaze m'm the tay-orn's gone in." She was a privileged old servant, withered, thin, and deeply marked with the smallpox; one of the old stamp, who had become withered in the service, and might say what she would, and had no difficulty or nervousness even with my grandfather himself. "Eh, Miss Jane," she would say to my aunt, when nervous, or distressed at some incisive or stern remark of her father's, " Eh, Miss Jane, ne'er heed him ! *I* ne'er heed him." In short, Millicent was a philosopher in addition to being cook for the time.

A few straggling houses down the beach and some fishing cottages behind, with one short wide street across, constituted the Lytham of those days. Consequently the society was limited, but what there was, was intimate, kindly, and friendly. Mrs. Fisher, benign and simple, was the lady benevolent of that period. Her parrot had been an intimate friend of mine in my eighth year, and my visits were generally spent with it in the kitchen. The jolting bathing machine on two wheels, with the two round holes out of reach, to let the light in, and the door fastened on the outside with a peg, continued to be by choice my grandfather's conveyance to church, though in these later days, being about eighty, he had a carriage with him, and took daily week-day drives—a stated distance on the same daily road.

RIGID SELF-RESTRICTION

He was daily to be seen at the same hour, seated in the bay-window with a parchment-bound portion of Mant and D'Oyley's Bible before him, in the same attitude, reading the small print of the notes without spectacles. The one o'clock dinner was followed by the punctual rest, and the punctual exercise after it; the renewed Bible study, and the tea at six, the prayers at eight, and the early bed-time; all things were done at a stated time, were punctual to the moment, and, without variation, were repeated as day succeeded to day, and months passed into years.

It was a singular close of life for one of powerful mind and strong judgment to adopt, and it deserves record as standing apart from the ordinary results of a successful career of active thought and enterprise. It may be allowed, perhaps, that its virtues lie rather in the austere than in the social code. An ascetic, with the possession of great wealth, he spent it not unfreely in the cause of public usefulness or charity, nor grudged it in any family abundance unconnected with parade. But he partook of no indulgences himself, practising a most rigid abstinence at an abundantly well-provided table—rejecting personally all luxury, all that could be termed in rigid judgment superfluities, all ordinary pleasures—secluding himself in the midst of a large and cheerful family, solemn in aspect, almost, perhaps, stern, pungent, sometimes withering in the few terse words he would bestow on any flippancy or extravagance, otherwise calm and mostly silent even in the short intervals when he joined the family circle—admitting none to close confidence, studying, evermore reading and reflecting, but seldom communicating, he naturally inspired in general more awe than affection, and, being looked upon from a distance, was often erroneously supposed to be morose. I have heard that his temper was irascible if provoked—*heard* only, for I never, through all my long experiences, saw him otherwise than calm—solemnly calm generally, yet some few times cheerfully, even humorously so. Sitting at the tea-table with the dry oat cake and the breakfast-cup of oatmeal porridge before him, or thoughtfully in the portico at Accrington House, on a summer's afternoon, watching the swallows that built within it, he would occasionally ask me a question in a kindly manner, which, if I had not been a little frightened simpleton, might easily have led to freer intercourse. He once said a thing which went direct to my heart. It was at this very period during my winter Lytham visit. Let me record it. He had a little relaxed his rigid rule of a dry flook (the commonest of Lytham fishes) and an equally dry rice pudding at dinner, and took some plain meat or game. My father had sent some partridges from Formby. With what tender feeling I looked upon those birds! I don't know how, or if, my grandfather found it out, or whether the shot were fired at random, but he said to me,

"Kitty"—he chose that name as the plainest, and always used it—"your Formby partridges are better than ours at Knowlmere.* I take it you have more corn than we have."

In the sudden flush of tender pride I enlarged, as diffusely as my courage would permit, upon the abundance of the sunny yellow fields of that so favoured land, and he listened good-humouredly, putting forward no contrasting plea for the heath-clad hills and rocky streams of his own land, with its many wild neighbouring beauties.

To conclude, I never heard of any deed of unkind-

* Knowlmere, in Yorkshire, is about three miles from Whitewell on one side, and a little further from the Trough of Bowland on the other.

ness laid to my grandfather's account; but I have heard of bountifully kind ones. Let me here reverently say, Be all respect and honour unto his memory! Ah me! I have attained, in these my later years, to a degree of sympathetic insight into the possible causes and motives of his uncustomary life, beyond what my philosophy dreamt of in those untried and untroubled days.

In the spring of the year I joined my parents at Seacombe, where we paused two or three weeks, preparatory to our departure for London. My Aunt Bessy was to accompany us, for the benefit of change and medical advice. She appeared to have suffered from the deep sadness of the home winter. From this date she became much altered. An ailment began to declare itself, which never left her. It caused discomfort and irritation without enough evident suffering to excite lasting sympathy—a state of things I have learnt, with larger experience, to feel for very differently from what I then did. What do the young and strong know of the weary wear of a continuous *mal-aise*?

We travelled leisurely post, stopping and diverging here and there for scenes of interest; and, arriving in London in April or early May, took up our abode there. The period of our London life, with its sorrowful conclusion, has been treated of in full in " Desultory Retracings," and I may pass over the next year or two cursorily. I went to school for awhile. A studious fever having followed too much anxiety for school honours in the end of 1833, convalesence was confirmed by the pleasant change of a fortnight in country air and freedom at Fairlawn. Here, too, it was the last experience of the old style. A few months later Eliza Yates was married, and Mr. Yates' death followed not long after, and a new era and order of things was inaugurated in that household, which had been to me one of the stabilities of the early life-dream, one of the places in which my childhood's associations had taken root, and of which, I had assumed, in the child fashion, a sort of arbitrary home possession.

Hitherto I had despised poetry with all the self-arrogated superiority of ignorance. My Godmother, Miss Yates, presented me with Scott's Poetical Works, in the early twelve volume edition. They opened my understanding and turned a wheel in the intellectual nature. What do not all the Queen's dominions owe to Sir Walter Scott!

Being well again, I returned to school in April for a final quarter, after which, my father had planned that we should travel awhile in Germany. Man proposeth, and God disposeth. A few days after the beginning of the summer vacation, my father was suddenly taken ill. A partial amendment took place, a startling worsening followed. I desire to pass over so painful a theme.* In little more than a fortnight from the first attack, he was laid in his grave; and my mother and myself, and Jane Watts were on our way, per mail, to Accrington, under the care of my uncle, Joe Peel, who had been sent by my grandfather on the instant, when the sad news had reached him.

Thus I grew up in two or three weeks—I do not mean to say that youth does not irresistibly recover itself, even from so grave a shock as this; but it would be ill if its after character had gained no depth through such a severe novitiate in sorrow.

My mother was struck down by the blow. She reached Accrington House only able to go to her own room, there to remain entirely secluded. Her desire was to go to Formby so soon as she should be able.

* This distressful period is more fully treated of in " Desultory Retracings."

THE MOURNFUL VISIT

She was now without anchor in life, and with no object to lead her in fixing on any place as a home. My brothers' course was in a measure settled, my brother Richard being already at Brazennose, and Henry about to enter on his college life there after the long vacation.

The first sorrowful weeks passed on slowly at Accrington where both my brothers joined us. In the early autumn we all went to Formby, arriving there under the first soreness of our own sad change, to feel, perhaps the more, how great the change there also. Our arrival could but add gloom to the settled gloom that already prevailed. On my part, I approached the old home of happiness with apprehension and nervousness, and a feeling of miserable strangeness in the very fact alone of looking for sorrow and not joy, and to a welcome of tears instead of smiles. Change! a change had come indeed! Within and without all was changed; the atmosphere was changed; the sunshine was changed, and did not dry up the autumnal dew that lay like tears on the seed-stems of the grass on the uncut lawn; the wind whistled drearily and moaned among the branches, and the withering leaves fell in melancholy consonance, the wood was lonely; the Bronc looked desolate.

> "Ah! Lady! we receive but what we give;
> And in our life alone doth Nature live."

True there were two new ponies; but how different from the pretty miniature bay, and the dear old grey that was no more! They were appropriately, though by accident, both black—by name, Raven and Jet; and my aunts were rather careful to make it understood they were established for health, and not for pleasure. My brothers' shirts needed refitting and renewing for College, and afforded an unwonted occupation as I sat upstairs with my mother in an unwonted room, into which I had hardly ever been in the happy days, except to peep under the covers at some old brocade amidst the shrouded furniture.

But I would pass shortly over this period. All its remembrances and circumstances are, even at this distance of time, too painful in their contrast to incline me to dwell upon them. Neither my aunts, nor ourselves, had yet fitted into our new position; nothing yet was natural or accustomed; the daily life was constrained; cheerfulness seemed out of place; yet cheerfulness is natural to youth, and would at times bubble up and then check itself.

The autumn days, silent and grey, sharpening into chill, and shortening, blend themselves into my memories of this season of restraint. Ere they had sharpened into winter, my brothers both repaired to College. My mother still shrank from the effort of establishing a home, and she, and I, and Jane Watts returned to Accrington. I was not sorry—there was no change at Accrington House, and it seemed most home where things were just the same as they had ever been.

But at Accrington too it was the last time that the old well-accustomed life would be found; the breaking-up was very close at hand, and that old familiar course which had seemed in childhood's estimation fixed and unalterable almost as the rising and the setting of the sun, was to pass into another phase for awhile, and then die out. I estimate its memory, perhaps, more highly than I did its possession.

> "It so falls out
> That what we have we prize not to the worth
> Whiles we enjoy it; but being lack'd and lost,
> . . . . Why then we find
> The virtue that possession would not shew us
> Whiles it was ours."

As I look upon its long familiarity, its fixity and sameness, I recognize in it an anchor to lean on awhile, as reflection reviews the shifting ways and fashions of more modern habits. And in these days when all things, places, and people are undergoing a metamorphosis, and change succeeds to change, and nothing is long of one stay, is there not a sense of repose in thus turning back for a moment to rest the mental eye once more on an even stretch of regularity and sameness, on a uniform motion like that of the sea, with the even ebb and flow of daily repetition—Is there not a repose to the spirit?

"Only the scholar knoweth (the limitation is a mistake) how deep a charm lies in monotony, in the old associations, the old ways, and habitual clockwork of peaceful time."—*The Caxtons.*

The old accustomed order, the old familiar faces, the well known and long habituated — there is a soothing, restful refreshment in the recall of these things. I feel it at this moment, as, once again, I sit, in memory, in the winter twilight, the fitful blaze of the fire lightening and darkening the window frames, and the steady rain streaming down the panes, while the composure of that still life of old steals upon me. The old armchair, the footstool with its tarnished gilt and its faded tassels, the oft-considered hand-screens on the chimneypiece, —in themselves a quaint history—the mirror that reflected true, and the opposite one that dwarfed us all into pigmies, with all the long succession of diminishing reflected rooms repeated in it ; these and other household shapes, picture, jar, cabinet, and the like, scanned and re-scanned in idle hours, rise for the moment into calm existence before me, so blended as these home things ever are—so much more so than we often recognize—with the inner history, with the ways and habits that build up the family character, and make the distinctive home life. Calm and sober monotony! what then passed, perhaps little noted, or noted as but dull repetition, has now all the sweet savour and the dignity of the long past and the never-to-be-renewed.

And, after all, have we not more root in the past than in the present? Did we not grow in it, and by it, to be what we are, and shall hereafter be? Does it not belong to us with infinite closeness? Is it any wonder that we look back upon it with an undying interest? Its customs and habits have tinctured the present. Its joys, its griefs, and its wearinesses lie far behind fair and smooth in the retrospective glow, and ourselves in the present are softened by the reflection they cast.

"Hath not old custom made our life more sweet?"

Old custom, indeed! What is there not in that custom? What gives nations and peoples dignity, and patriots devotion, but a past? What gives poetry to the ruined castle or abbey, but a past? What makes America what it is but the want of it? "The God of Abraham, Isaac and Jacob, the God of your fathers." What a solemn appeal to the past! "Walk in the old paths." "Ask of the days of old." There is wisdom in them, mellowed wisdom, mellowed beauty. Time beautifies the memory of good with its moss and its ivy, and softens its harsher lines, crumbling them into a kindly indistinctness, and then colours all with sober variety of venerable hues; and our eye is taught, and our taste refined, and our spirit chastened, and our soul soothed, by the contemplation and the study of the mouldering structure in its unimpassioned majesty and beauty.

CHAPTER II

> " Young Fancy, oft in rainbow vest array'd
> Points to new scenes that in succession pass
> Across the wond'rous mirror that she bears,
> And bids the unsated soul and wandering eye
> A wider range o'er all her prospects take."
> —*H. Headley.*

April 11th, 1867.

As I advance further into more mature memories I find that yet more variety enters into them. The one well-spring of love and hope in the child heart, as it flowed on into a stream, necessarily received contributions from other sources, and also branched out its waters into other and distinct channels.

Insensibly as years passed, and the powers of appreciation developed, other places, other people, and other interests mingled in with the one absorbing fulness of child-devotion to the one centre, and, therefore, these later records can no longer be so chiefly confined to their one first object.

I closed my last chapter with our return to Accrington House, and the foreshadowing of the change in store, even for the seemingly assured and invariable course that had run on there, in even regularity, from the dawn of my consciousness.

Nothing under this our sun can continue ever in one stay. All must bow to the law of change. So, at the close of the sadly solemn year of 1834 in my life history, closed the reign of law at Accrington House by the death at Lytham of its Head.

I have told in greater fulness in "Desultory Retracings" of the death of my grandfather Peel, and there entered fully into its consequences as leading my mother to fix her abode in the Lytham Cottage, so convenient to ourselves in many ways, and, especially so, as Accrington could be reached from it in a few hours, and there was easy access to Formby, in summer, at least, across the river to Southport, and through the sandy lanes and sand-hill track, from thence to the skirts of the wood at the back of the Hall; or, otherwise, all by land round by Liverpool.

Thus I pass on with but a slight touch over the first year of our Lytham life and its events, however important eventually to my own future.

"All the rivers run into the sea, yet the sea is not full: unto the place from whence the rivers come, thither they return again."

And so the Ribble ran its course, and tides ebbed and flowed again on the shingle and on the sand, and so flowed the even course of our life, my mother living apart in her great sorrow, and seeing no one. My Aunt Jane Peel, who remained with us the first year or so, found satisfaction in the quiet interest of gardening, maintaining the flower-border in such order that her friends declared she watched each flower as it threatened to fade, since not so much as a fallen rose-leaf ever marred its perfect neatness, nor was one blade of grass to be seen above its fellows on the shaven lawn. If my part was mostly to criticize or admire, yet I was not unreadily bribed to undertake the more laborious offices of trimming and nailing; and thus, in peaceful occupation, varied with "books and work and healthful play," the summer of 1835 came upon us.

Whether the narrowed channel of our life contracted, or the enlarged capacities of my own mind

FIRST VISIT TO BARTON

confuse my memory, and amalgamate events, I do not know, but I have no longer before me the clearly defined sequence of every movement and change. I can no longer chronicle each Formby visit, and each distinguishing event of each, with the infallibility of heretofore. I may even soon be compelled to refer to written notes. Hitherto I had been guiltless of note making on paper, and those in the memory are by far the best defined.

This our first Lytham summer brought the ordinary moderate tide of sea-side visitors, amongst others the family from Barton, and Charlotte and Fanny Jacson became the first friends of my own standing I had ever had. This alliance was followed up by an autumn visit to the future home, so altogether unforeseen as such. There I was initiated into " society," serving my apprenticeship by taking my part in certain dinner parties, passing through the ordeal with the embarrassment and alarm considered, in the twilight portion of this enlightened century, not wholly unbecoming " sweet seventeen.'

In the winter that quickly followed I went to Formby, strange to say the first time I had ever seen it in winter bareness. Ah! the old sweetness! how it reasserted itself, spite of all metamorphoses. How sweet were the voices of past summers by the winter fires. Evidently my aunts had resolved to make an effort to return, at least in some measure, to the old life, and to open the doors again to cheerfulness and innocent enjoyment. They assembled that Christmas, a party of nephews and nieces, encouraged their merriment, and, to the amazement of the stuffed birds, and the dark pictures, in celebration of my eighteenth birthday, chalked the slippery floors of the entrance hall, caused a crackling fire to blaze in the astonished fire-place, and promoted a dance.

That Christmas-tide was bright and exhilarating, decked out, as it was, in frost jewellery; I and my cousins walked on the Bronc when the frozen snow lay crisp on its level surface, and cracked beneath our feet; and the sun sank among glowing clouds behind the sandhills in the early afternoon hours; and there, stirred by opening influences, I made my first ventures in expressing thoughts, opinions, or impressions on subjects which I had hitherto only pondered upon alone. By the glow of those winter sunsets streaming over the wide level from the vast and gorgeous cloud and sky, it came more easily, though with blushes, to venture into the straight walks in the outskirts of "divine philosophy"; hazarding opinion or surmise on practical themes, moral and social; not yet intruding with presumptuous step into the "clueless labyrinths" of the speculative and conjectural; nor, as yet, daring or caring to embark in "rudderless balloons to drift after the phantasms of reverie."

Amongst the group of Formby relatives assembled on that pleasurable occasion, William Peel, of Culham, took part—an after-life's sojourn at Natal, I find, has not obliterated its pleasurableness from his memory.

Lonsdale, he whom my aunts delighted to honour, and others of my Uncle John's family were chief in the number—the young men were in the habit of spending the Sunday frequently with their aunts. Lonsdale was spoken of then, by them, and treated markedly with a certain grave distinction, which made one understand the position they regarded him as occupying.

In other respects my memory of this winter visit is not peculiarly vivid—I chiefly recognize its especial charm in the novel privilege of sitting up late with my Aunt Mary in the dining-room. We did not talk in these late evening hours. She was generally occupied with executor papers and accounts, and I read, and, after my fashion, analyzed Butler's Analogy; but the charm lay in being with her, in that privileged companionship, though silent.

From Formby I went to my uncle's* at Sandon Terrace, there to contract a long, a life-long debt of affection and gratitude for tenderness and home welcome which knew no chill or change in all after years, and grew to be part of the heart's daily bread all through and beyond the period of youth, being so recognized in fulness then as much as now—a peculiarity on which I reflect with pleasure.

It was in February or March of that spring that I went with Sophia Peel, under the guardianship of Miss Wallace, to pay a visit to my godmother, Miss Yates, at Fairlawn. The inexorable changes of death and marriage had recently left her alone; a slight and fragile woman, not perhaps exactly young, but neither as yet elderly—blind—the sole indweller of the place. A pleasant place in truth it was, standing, serene and spacious, within and without, in the sunshine and fertility of garden Kent: a mansion known in the historic times of Cromwell, and supposed to be at this time, as formerly, haunted in the old part by the headless ghost of Sir Harry Vane; but in the main body of the house, which had been rebuilt after a fire at a later period, as free from spectral horror as light, and space, and luxurious comfort could make any place. My associations with it were all of pleasure from the earliest stage when, at seven years old, I fished and shot rooks, and sat in the stable during April showers with Jonathan Yates, then lately free

* Richard Formby, M.D. He was the third son of my grandfather. He resided during his professional life in Liverpool, taking the lead in the medical line with Dr. Brandreth. He was Physician to the Infirmary and Lecturer on Anatomy.

from Oxford ; and churned little pats of butter, and held tea parties with the maids and Jane Watts in the sewing-room when he was from home.

Let not even child gratitude wholly die out. I will not pass on without a backward glance, now gravely and affectionately given, to the good natured friend and associate of those pleasant earliest Fairlawn days. At my first arrival I looked upon Jonathan Yates, a grown up man, with awe as ranking among the gods, whom I could only approach with obeisance. He, no doubt, had stooped to raise up the little serf at his feet, for at breakfast one day, very shortly after our arrival, I found myself confiding to him the secret horrors of the dark ; adding, concerning a grinning monkey as seen on a window ledge halfway up the stairs, " But then, you know, I don't suppose it was really there." His remark on this disclaimer of too ready credulity I remember in its very words:

" Well now," said he, quite as if he meant it, " if I had seen it, I should believe it *was* really there."

With a great opening out of assurance I crept up close to him, and the converse proceeded in a confidential undertone. From that propitious hour awe melted into delight and partnership, and I attached myself to him with the unreserved love of early seven. The three horses, Sweed, Noah, and the slim thoroughbred chestnut, the terrier Myrtle, the fishing rods, the Eau-de-Cologne bottle, and all his other belongings became, in a reflected sense, mine ; and every rook he shot was a personal distinction to myself.

There were at Fairlawn certain fish preserves and ponds ; and fishing was a favourite pastime with Jonathan, and one which I was invariably allowed to share. One bright breezy April morning, in preparation for the day's sport, he was arranging some flies on the library table before an open window, while I stood by, intently watching the process with a delighted sense of its importance. A servant happening to enter, the draught scattered the flies all around on the carpet. Jonathan's exclamation, "that it was enough to make a parson swear!" seemed to me the wittiest thing imaginable, and I repeated it to myself many times afterwards, finding a certain glory in it; and, recalling it now to mind, there comes with it the breezy freshness of that April morning blowing into the room from over the fair lawn.

It was not that I felt the utterance in itself commendable, but it approached the boundary of forbidden excesses, and so had a spicy savour of masculine indemnity. The gods on their Olympic heights, I had long discerned, had mysterious privileges that the uninitiated did not participate in. I concluded that they were raised above the laws which bound child morality; or that, in some way, that which appeared to be was not.

Such is the faith of childhood, and a pity it is it should ever be misled or imposed upon.

Jonathan Yates was my first correspondent: I regret that the correspondence was not preserved. I saw him but once again before his early death; but that was in Paris, where apart from the joys of stable and fishing rods, there was lack of community in interests and pursuits, and seven years old is more companionable and adventurous than ten.

Still, looking back to the earlier time, it pleases me to pay this slight passing tribute to a young man's good-natured kindness.

I have slipped aside into these earlier retrospects; slipped aside from the trimmer garden scenery into the cowslip fields and the bluebell brakes and copsewoods as I remember them in the childish days. I recall myself, and return to the well-kept walks through the cultivated pleasure grounds—youth's pathway instead of childhood's ; but lying in sunshine as bright ; I will not stop to enquire whether as soft and dewy—but surely leading away from the simpler charms of the primrose dell and wild rose hedgerow, to more artificial beauties and interests ; to another order of enjoyments, in short, with less of impersonality, more of complacency in them.

To a guest thus treading as it were without thought or care on velvet and rose leaves ; it was an interlude in life, pleasant enough so long as no questions as to its moral worth and productiveness rose up in the mind to trouble it. Probably none at the actual time did so rise up ; for its memory turns on no grating hinge. Ease and favour reigned within ; the world paid court ; and meanwhile, outside, beyond the drawing room and orangery atmosphere, fresh spring winds blew over rich lands, and spring sunshine broke out upon flowers, and verdure, and luxuriance.

Our Lytham Cottage was wanted by the owner, which caused us to migrate in 1836 for a year, the first six months of which we spent under the wing of Penmaen Mawr, at Plas Uchaf.

It has been my lot, I find, to know places on the eve of change. I made my first acquaintance with that tract of hill and sea, now a place of so much resort, when it was almost a desolate solitude, unconscious of a visitor, or inn, or lodging-house beyond the " Jolly Herring," and the " New Shop " at the foot of the mountain road up to Plas Uchaf. It was there I first learnt anything of the influences of hill and valley, and of the rugged and grand in nature. Perhaps, then, the direct effects were more those of bodily exhilaration in the delight of getting to the top of places, than of mental elevation; the joys of scrambling, in short, rather than the joys of contemplation. Yet the solitude of the mountain moorland, and the majesty of rock and sea, were not without their latent powers, even at that time of super-abundant animal vigour that was hardly to be quieted into receptiveness.

In the autumn when my brothers had returned to Oxford we went, according to pre-arrangement, to Fairlawn for the winter. In my mother's case, however, so great a change of habit proved quite too overpowering, and I was left alone to the advantages, real or supposed, of an introduction into wider and higher social spheres than our secluded life brought within reach.

Wealth, ability and culture, liberal hospitality, and the peculiarity of blindness, made Miss Yates an object of note and interest. The charm of what the neighbours termed "her hospitable mansion" lay in its excellent domestic arrangement. The punctuality was that of Accrington, but it ran more softly, in more polished grooves, amid the perfume and garnish of more worldly grace and gratification. Gaudy annuals, and books of beauty, and new publications of other sorts, lay on the tables amid conservatory flowers; guests flowed in and out, and high-sounding names mixed in the daily converse.

For awhile all this was pleasant; but, as in the well-trimmed and ornamental groves and gardens without, one presently reached the limit, and felt the restraint of it.

> "Vain art, vain hope! 'tis fruitless all,
> At length we reach the boundary wall;
> And, sick of flower and trim dress'd tree,
> Long for rough glade and forest free."

In the February we returned to Lytham, taking

a temporary lodging there till we should determine where next to fix ourselves. It so happened at the very time, that a little feminine changeableness in the feelings of its fresh occupants set our pretty cottage at liberty, and we closed with the opportunity, and re-engaged it, glad of any leading to help in determining our final choice of residence. We had also the advantage of some improvements in added space and ornament.

The little abode was pretty and convenient, and cheerful, and protected; and there, once again, my mother decided to settle; and, being settled, took root and stayed finally, witnessing by year the outspreading of the place, east, west, and north, till it lost entirely all claim to seclusion.

I will now for a moment advert to those quiet episodes in life, when, as for instance, in a tour of pleasure, we have sat on the rock, or the wild thyme bank, by the lake, or the river, at the close of the day, and felt, rather than seen, the overwatching presence of the near mountains in the twilight and silence; and have been drawn on to meditation or converse on themes that becalm and exalt the mind. Even likewise, thus softening and purifying in the early journey of life, are the calm pleasures that grow out of friendship with our elders. The hours spent in freely confiding our young temerities to the willing ear of kindly sympathizing experience, have a grace of gravity and quietude akin to the hallowing pause of the evening hour in scenes of nature's beauty.

The link of affection that couples the young to the old is a golden one. I have known and valued the worth of this golden link in many instances, and would here bear an affectionate tribute to an unrestricted interchange of friendly communion with Mrs. Saunders,* which added pleasantness to several years of Lytham life.

It would lead me too far astray to enumerate all friends and sources of interest. But one other I cannot fail to mention; nor would it imply disrespect to name him in the same breath with any, even the much valued. I mean the dog Neptune, the gift of my uncle, Hesketh Formby; the once little Newfoundland puppy that arrived in a hamper on a summer's afternoon in 1838, and sat wincing and whining on our dress skirts, getting close for solace, and looking up in our faces and lamenting. How Jane nursed him; and how I disciplined, and taught, and delighted in him; and how my mother yielded to the common infection, and how he was distinguished beyond all other of dog kind, honoured and deferred to, privileged and chartered, exhibited and made famous, and publicly recognized as a great character.† How all this, and much more, of adulation, public and private; of appreciation and affection, were accorded to him, need I here tell? In all the after home life at the Lytham cottage he is mixed up. In long walks on shore or inland, sitting on the shingle or the sand-hill, alone with a book, or in quiet converse with a friend, he was guard and companion. Equally on the summer shore, or on the rug by the winter fire, he was a part of the daily life, a companion never out of favour, useful as a little foot-page in the baronial chamber, to pick up, to fetch, to carry; and better than many a graduate

---

*Mrs. Saunders, the mother of Mrs. Chas. Hesketh, of North Meols Rectory—our distant cousin by marriage; and of W. A. F. Saunders, of Wennington Hall. She died August, 1868, in her 86th year.

† See "Autobiography of Neptune," by Mrs. Burrows; and "Jesse's History of the British Dog."

in the higher arts, to comprehend and sympathize with mood or circumstance whatsoever. How indeed without the tribute of an allusion should I pass by so old and close a friend? Of horses, in which I dealt before his time with various ill turns of fate, I will here take no note.

There was nothing about Lytham to feed, far less satisfy, the sense of the picturesque or the poetic. The river mouth has not the roll, the roar, and the stretch of the ocean. The quiet of a sparely-frequented watering place has not the grand characteristics, the "dreadful pleasures" of a solitude. Lytham was in all points the embodiment of unmarked and respectable commonplace; good in many ways; for do not our ordinary duties, and even pleasures, lie much in commonplace? and good in this way, that scenes of higher interest met a warmer appreciation from the force of contrast—and of such contrast I proceed to give an instance.

My mother arranged that we should make an excursion to the Lakes. Those were yet the days of posting. We were to call at Barton for Fanny Jacson, who was to be my companion.

We set out from Lytham in moderately early morning; it was late in the spring of (I think) 1838, posted on all day, through pouring rain, arriving at Bowness in the evening in a swathe of cloud. I had never seen anything of Lake kind beyond an inland county mere; and, in that sort of youthful perverseness which rather prides itself in depreciating what is accredited as worthy, I looked down upon the Lakes from the scoffing altitude of ignorance, deeming them of the nature of show places; like parks, or grottoes, suggestive of cockneyism.

The dense rain having prevailed all day, we saw

little but the roadsides on our journey ; and, still seeing little else, the carriage drew up all dripping at Ullock's Hotel, a rough-cast house, bearing a sign overhanging the door ; if I remember right, of a white hart. The inn was a charming inn ; that was not to be denied; charming then from its homeliness. There was to be seen from its window, from beneath a verandah, a little square terrace of green and flowers, and, below that, some smooth water; and, around all, a mist. We were in cloud-land assuredly, and it was pleasant enough so to find oneself; but, so far, there was no conversion, for in point of fact there was nothing as yet to produce it; no especial beauty or grandeur to warrant rapture, no lake, no mountains, only a pretty little wet space about us, standing out in a vague domain of water and cloud. Tea with trout, in a pleasant little parlour on a terrace in a cloud, was charming as a change; but not all-powerful to convert an unbeliever in lake loveliness to the true faith.

It rained all night, and the aspect of things was precisely the same the next morning. The grassy little terrace was very fresh, and the flowers and the ferns, surcharged with rain drops, were also very fresh, and even bright looking and cheerful in their cloud clothing, being native to it, and to the manner born ; but all other beauties were necessarily matter of faith only: the little stretch of lake, visible, melted within a stone's throw, undefinedly, into the all-embracing cloud which for the present bounded our prospect. We were not quite satisfied to sit all day even in the pretty terraced parlour ; and we ordered a boat, took umbrellas and wrappings, and set forth to penetrate the cloud, and look beyond our boundaries. We sat shrouded in our draperies like daughters of the mist ; the boatmen rowed on, the rain fell straight down, dappling the water, the cloud was as dense as ever, there was not a breath of wind, silence reigned except for the plash of the oars and of the large rain-drops. Still we rowed on; and then all at once there broke forth a great change. It was the third day of rain: and that, they said, was the Lake allotment. The mourning was over, and the oil of joy was ready to out-pour itself. The dropping on the lake ceased, a flush of warmth followed, and a line of gold colour crept over the mist, and then it broke into pathways, and rolled into wreaths and clouds; a sky of the clearest blue came to light in patches, and purple mountain tops with sudden sunshine on them appeared above the cloud wreaths; the lake, which was as even as a sheet of glass, reflected these great and high and bright glories, and also every fragile branch, and leaf, and blade of grass, and straggling fern, that hung over the bank of the island near us, as faithfully as the best polished mirror might have done—a poor and inadequate image; for how can a mirror render those subtle effects of warmth, of silence, of sound, of placidity, of contrast, and of harmony? effects to which the inner mind or spirit is so mysteriously attuned. And yet Shelley gives it so much grace that I cannot forbear adding his beautiful lines—

> "Sweet views, which in our world above
>   Can never well be seen,
> Were imaged by the water's love
>   Of that fair forest green;
>
> And all was interfused beneath
>   With an Elysian glow;
> An atmosphere without a breath,
>   A softer day below."

It was indeed an indescribable wealth of loveliness and of glory that opened out in that hour, above, below, and around. There were the copper beeches, the brown oaks, the light green larches and elms, in the many hues of early June; the breadths of blue sky, and the soft thunder-clouds gathering in the far distance; the white wreaths of mist floating about the valley, the purple, and the brown, and the violet, and the gold of mountain height, and of cloud, and of sky-line; the dark rock rising out of the sunny green of meadow and woodland; and the rivulet and mountain stream gleaming and glancing in the light. There lay the rugged and the smooth, the soft and the grand, all entranced in the deep calm. The boatmen rested on their oars, and the trout rose at the May-flies, and the distant thrush sang from the mainland woods—And the suddenness of it all! It was as if a curtain had been drawn aside, revealing to a new sense a new world. I had never imagined such loveliness—my conversion was instantaneous, was complete, was deep, was lasting. Among the many and various beauties of our own beautiful country with which other and later years have made me familiar, this, the scene of my first insight and experience of the power that these external things can exercise upon us, stands out yet prominent.

There are scenes in Scotland more imposing; in Wales more extensive; the Irish lakes are larger; and among our own I have thought others more lovely and more impressive; yet, after so thinking and saying, when I have returned to Windermere, and caught a favourable hour, looking up to its water-head in the varying gleam of shadow, of sunshine, and cloud, I have returned to the impression that, well known, oft seen, made common as it is now to the million, yet, surely, was never aught more fair!

That hour of sudden disclosure is indeed a sweet remembrance, and from it one might evolve parables, and analogies of the moral law, as to the enhancing of all joys and successes when they develope out of sorrows, difficulties, and other obscurities of moral cloud and rain.

With this vision of radiant beauty glistening in its diamonds, and laughing after its tears, rises at this moment, from the caprice of memory, or the power of contrast, another scene, beautiful of its kind, even very beautiful, but unprized, or rather felt almost painfully at the time, and not laid up with store of gracious perfumes in the chambers of remembrance. It was on the banks of the Wye, in a year of very gorgeous autumnal colouring, on the 1st of November, when the woods were crimson, and orange, and russet, the sky unclouded, and dust on the road. On the Windermere lake on the early summer day, Youth was at the prow and Pleasure at the helm. Looking, in graver years, upon the winding Wye in the pomp of all that autumnal glory, anxious doubts and theological difficulties disquieted and burdened the spirit, and the beauty of external things lay oppressively upon it. Coleridge is right, the life of nature is but reflected from our own. In one mood, we say, How much lies in these things! in another, Ah, how little!

So far as I catch the clue to the contradiction; in joy, or when the mind is receptive, whether placid, or saddened, or touched with pleasing melancholy, external nature plays upon an inner chord of exceeding sweetness; in tumult, anxiety, or apprehension, its serene indifference mocks our disquietude, and aggrieves us.

But for this latter experience I think I might have fallen into a sort of idolatry or Pantheistic worship, deeming the witching power of the mountain, the wild thyme bank, or the primrose clump, to be inherent in the inanimate things themselves, as a subtle inner life and spirit capable of communing with our spirit. Visions and dreams of fancy! A fascinating bewilderment! "In this also is vanity."

I have alluded to the Lytham life of earlier days. I think I ought to add a reference to the pretty cottage of this period, before it passes away altogether from my own rightful interest in it as my mother's home. It was always a pleasing object, embowered in its few trees, whether seen from beach or river, in near or distant view; for its trellised roses had never a straggling branch, nor its shaven lawn a blade of green out of place; its flower border was immaculate, and the greenhouse, verandah, and bay window, bedecked with their geraniums and flowering plants which my mother carefully watched over, were the perfection of neatness and good taste. I think it can in no way be so fairly described as by calling it "a little picture"; and the order within equalled the neatness without. Whether in summer with verandah and greenhouse doors open, or in winter with the two bright fires blazing opposite, nothing could better personify cheerfulness than its two sitting-rooms when the folding doors were thrown open, or snugness when they were closed. If I place my mother on her little rocking-chair reading "The Times," and suppose Jane Watts knocking at the door and entering with an egg of some peculiarity of shape or size, a beaming face, and "you'll 'scuse me, ma'am," I shall have before me a sketch of the home interior from the life.

How natural it is in making a record of a life, or a series of sketches, to take the salient points and to pass over the monotony and common-place, the wet days and the contrarieties; and hence a retrospect may suggest a course of more even satisfaction and peacefulness than would have been always acknowledged in the daily reality; and I must confess that the picture I am drawing of the untroubled life in those two comfortable rooms recommends itself as more enjoyable in memory than it was, at all times, wont to do in possession. And yet I was always very thankfully sensible of its comforts; but Lytham, as a place, did not ever really engage my affections. The cottage itself must be dear from its home associations; and, as I dwell on those, I feel that the right to its tenure will now, alas! be short; and sadness checks further description.

Of course, the home life was varied with excursions and visits of which I do not attempt to make any record. I might instance this, my present home;* I might touch on Ince, near Chester, as a place having to myself associations by no means trivial ; but I will not wander into labyrinths where I might lose the clue for return.

Such are some of the varying scenes and sketches that memory repictures. I think I have inwoven them in my record that I might turn with the greater warmth, with the more tenderness, with the old speciality of heart love to the legitimate object of these my youth's reminiscences. Ah! and now, turning to it in a time of increased illness and anxiety, I welcome the more its soothing power. Let me stand once again in life-like memory, with the heart of youth, before the oriel door-way, on the drive dented with the marks of the ponies' feet, as the sun shines on the creamy whiteness of those dear walls. I see the beech boughs stretching over, and the light flickering through them on those hoof marks, and my heart is thrilled, and my spirit soothed. I see the side-saddled ponies being led through the deep shade of the gate-way that shuts out the stable and farm buildings. I hear my aunts'

* Barton Hall, five miles from Preston.

voices near the mounting block, the broad stump of the noble old ash tree; I see my Aunt Mary, with whip or extra cape in hand, coming to assist at the mounting and arrange the habit-skirt to the stirrup; I hear the voice, I see the smile, I recall the atmosphere of sunshine and peace; and, being weak, I could weep with tenderness.

CHAPTER III

"Audi alteram partem."

July, 1873.

A long interval here intervenes consequent on a prolonged breakdown which cut short the recording power. A stroke from a foreign hand gave the impetus to resume the work long laid by. It came from Nathaniel Hawthorne, the American romanticist, among the last, one would have supposed, to concern himself with the Formby sandhills.

And it came in the following way:—

On a hot afternoon, turning over carelessly the pages of a book by Nathaniel Hawthorne, the idle eye was quickened into attention by catching sight of certain familiar names.

On August 24th, 1856, he (Nathaniel Hawthorne) "took the rail by Liverpool for Southport," (consequently passing through the outskirts of Formby). "The ride," says he, "is through a most uninteresting tract of country . . . the railway skirts along the sea the whole distance, but is shut out from the sight of it by the low sandhills which seem to have been heaped up by the waves . . . I have not seen a drearier landscape even in Lancashire." And, later on, during a few months' residence in Southport, he says, "The country about Southport has as few charms as it is possible for any region to have. In the close neighbourhood of the shore it is nothing but sandhills covered with coarse grass."

Coarse grass! let me, in the first place, correct the error of ignorance. Mr. Hawthorne, evidently, is not a botanist. He is wholly unconscious that this "coarse grass"—correctly "sea reed "*—this lover of the free ocean breeze, unique specimen, in this country, of its genus, is cultivated with care, having an especial value peculiar to itself, as a guardian power. For by its singularly long stretching roots it binds the loose sand, and protects, from desolating drifts of it, the pastoral plain of grass and arable land which stretches along the discredited belt of sand-hills.

Nothing but sand hillocks covered with this same sea reed! One cannot controvert it. No, nothing more. Nothing except the incommunicable *what?* that gives characteristic life to everywhere—to that which is "nothing more" than running water among stones, the witchery of the babbling brook; to the "yellow primrose" on its brink, that which stirs "thoughts that lie too deep for tears"; or to that which is "nothing more" than a great heap of earth and rock, the majesty of the mountain.

Nothing but sand, and sea, and solitude, in sea-breeze and sunshine. Nothing but the sea-bird's cry, and the swift scutter of the little conies that harbour there, to break the silence and give motion to the stillness of an isolation, as complete for the time as that of the Arabian desert. No, one cannot deny the imputation. No, nothing more than these.

Stay! let the ungracious announcement pass with an excuse. To all, not all is given. True, Mr. Hawthorne is a writer of fiction, of romances, read and lauded; but Mr. Hawthorne is an American. If, in truth, his place be high among the imaginative and perceptive, yet his birth shuts him out from one sense that involves much; there is one

* Or by other botanists, " sea-sedge."

voice missing in the intellectual scale—a voice of solemn depth, and tender sweetness—

"Land of my sires!"

No answering thrill of heart, no irrepressible tear of tenderness starts to the apostrophe!

There must be a fine sensitive chord altogether lacking among the tuneable strings of that heart, which the mysterious influences of the long past have never made silent, at times, with a solemn emotion beyond words.

"I have not seen a drearier landscape even in Lancashire." I am tickled by the pitiless verdict. There is a humorous incongruity in the convex and concave view of a matter. I once at Lodore overheard a stout gentleman, with his hands in his pockets, questioning a driver who was cleaning his car, as to where he had come from that day. "What!" he exclaimed, as the man designated his course over a glorious stretch of mountain, including the wild abrupt height of Honister Crag, "What! over that nasty crag!" The day before, I and others had passed by that same crag, touched to the soul with the grand poetry of the scene—I, for one, in youth's enthusiasm, almost a worshipper of its glorious desolation made sweet by the summer softness.

The crag and its surroundings have certainly a more unassailable vantage-ground of refutation—yet if "the mountains bring peace," so also "the little hills righteousness unto the people," and viewed as for mere contemplative calm, and as aids to the mind "which meditates upon many things," I think that, possibly, the "little hills," in their summer solitude, may do their work of influence with less distracting superabundance than the more majestic mountains. Any way, strange, in a mind of the higher class, and with a leaning to the romantic, is the insensibility implied in this contemptuous sweeping aside of all claim to interest in a scene at least singular in its features, distinct in character, and isolated from the common-place.

"No drearier landscape even in Lancashire." One is disposed to refer this insensibility, this unresponsiveness to the companionship of the unpeopled, this unconsciousness of minor individualities of scenic character, to the result of a brobdignag habit of vision cognizant mainly of Niagarean effects, and so unadapted to the niceties of subtler essences.

Size and newness do not spiritualize, and, perhaps, physical expansion tends somewhat to the overshadowing of the psychological element. It is true that, now, size and newness very much influence taste and judgment. Cabbages the size of hollybushes, flowers the size of cabbages, carry the day, and no ugliness or monstrosity meets objection if only the extravagance be new. But this development of progress had hardly unfolded itself in the period of Nathaniel Hawthorne's passage through the Formby sandhills. Any way, there is something short of the complete in the author and romanticist, who sees not the quiver of the atmosphere, playing in the sunlight, between the yellow sand and the blue sky, nor hears the lullaby of the distant surge in the sleep of the noon, when even the harebells are unstirred among the wild-flower oases of this miniature desert—who has owned to no bounding of heart in meeting the breeze over the wide level of solitary shore, and solitary sea—a shore without a footprint, and a sea without a sail. So, at least, it used to be. In the stretch of shore and sea from the lifeboat-house at Formby Point, till within a mile or two of the mouth of the Ribble at Southport, it was a rare thing to see even a sign of human life. Time after time, in those joyous past-days' excursions to the shore for riding or bathing, we went and returned through the sunny solitudes, with no human trace, either in sound or sight, save in those sharp-cut and long-remaining tracks of the ponies' feet, left from former passings in the moist sand of those watery levels which diversify the home wilderness.

All this, I suppose, has now undergone a change. No doubt, when railway trains shoot past, and stations and villas dot the line, must the individuality be destroyed. Too surely must the spirit have departed, and the charm be dispelled. And now that the contemplative calm of the scene, and the rustic simplicity of the people are gone together, Hawthorne, for what I know, may be justified; and, possibly, "even in Lancashire," to such as are not under the spell of the old enchantment, there may be "no drearier region" than the Formby sand land.

Pause here, however, and hear, once again, "the other side." Let the writer of the extract, taken from a source not unduly to be suspected of romantic excesses, viz., the "Manchester Guardian," bear his testimony as follows:—

"The ordinary traveller who journeys by the Lancashire and Yorkshire Railway will be surprised at the poetry which mere sandhills can inspire . . . The writer we have here quoted states that 'within the broadest portion of the range of sandhills, shut out entirely from the outer world, lies a series of fresh water lakes, many acres in extent, which are most charmingly wild and picturesque—the fantasy of nature has here described, in wildest beauty, all the geographical features of seas, bays, islands, and peninsulas, with a delightfully broken surface of irregular hills and plains, where mosses and aquatic plants revel . . . The water, which is most pellucid, is the haunt of waterfowl, which are seldom disturbed in this beautiful solitude.'"

In addition to this, indisputably, impartial confirmation of all I may ever have said myself of the

THE SAND HILLS.

charm which lies hidden in these scenes, I will add the written remark of a stranger to the soil, though a sojourner.

Alluding to the place, he says, " In the wild parts, I have seen and felt it to be so beautiful, that I have felt quite thankful to God for making it so lovely and wild."

But I—independently of all conflicting opinions —I, casting back a glance upon my world that was, calling back to life what someone calls "the sacred, tender, intangible spirit of the past," I remain faithful to the early spell; and, rehearsing the sense of soul contentment, known there ever, and there in fulness only, my heart is watered, and my faith in all that is good is refreshed.*

For there—let me record it, if I do but repeat myself—let me record it, as a tribute due from the thirsty soil to the rain that has watered it—there all the sweet influences of my life have had their birth, —there was the central point from which all sweet remembrances issued, and to which every thought or impulse of good tended as to its home. Hope strained towards it, Faith found rest in it, Love flew to it as to its own home. In all these long later years of very painful experience, these years of compulsory thinking, and of mental trial in inaction, throughout all the varying struggle, the re-living memories of the Formby days have had an unfailing power to soothe and upraise, and throughout, has that home of the deep, if simple, joys of the child soul been ever the true type of Heaven.

* "For the perfect and permanent repose of the heart we want one to love—above us, so that reverence may mingle with esteem— like us, so that closely and familiarly we may embrace one in whom all conceivable excellencies meet and centre, all that the eye covets to admire, that the heart asks to love."—*Hanna's* "*Ministry in Galilee.*"

Yes, why should I not write it as I have a thousand and a thousand times thought it, and felt it, and realized it as between my soul and its Maker; that place, in which it was given to the child to realize the calm of complete happiness, has taught me to understand the nature of Heaven, where the "soul shall be satisfied even as it were with marrow and fatness," and where, in the presence of the One who fulfils all its desire, is "the fulness of joy."

The presence of the Beloved; the surrounding of all that is high, excellent, beautiful, soul-satisfying, constitute Heaven. That is at once the most scriptural, and the most reasonable conception of it. And if it were the child-soul that most realized it, it has not the less of Gospel sanction for that.

Among the choicest of God's gifts to me, that child-love and worship of what was, to it, the fulness of all beauty and excellence, is, perhaps, the very choicest.

I copy the following roughly scrawled on a loose bit of paper during an attack of scarlet fever in 1869, in a very tottering hand:—

"When left alone, I go to the seat in the wood and sit there again by Aunt Mary, with the fresh-scratched rabbit hole by our side." That love for her—I know nothing to equal it. It was the most perfect culmination of purity, of sweetness, of innocence, and of devotion.

"Whatsoever things are pure and lovely, think on them," says the Apostle. I cannot obey the behest better than thus recalling that love.

If this seem fanciful or exaggerated to other minds, it is their error. I wrote this, in the first instance, for myself alone. Should I try to play false with myself? Well known to myself is its truth, its simple genuine reality, its long-tried, well-proved, heartfelt conviction of inward experience. In the calm certainty of its truth I thank God!

Have I not then a right to love. Nay, would it not be a baseness not to love, and to love deeply—

> " This land of such dear souls,
> This dear, dear land ! "
> —*Richard II.*

even " to favour the dust thereof " ?—For,

> " What if earth
> Be but the shadow of Heaven, and things therein
> Each to the other like, more than on earth be thought ? "

CHAPTER IV

> " A Being breathing thoughtful breath,
> A traveller between life and death;
> The reason firm, the temperate will,
> Endurance, foresight, strength, and skill:
> A perfect woman, nobly planned."
> —*Wordsworth.*

March, 1897.

This memorial being chiefly drawn from youthful records, I feel there will be a deficiency without a final endorsement from the judgment of latest age. Also, since the dedicating page refers especially to the memory of Mary Formby, the last survivor of the three sisters, I feel it will be befitting to give in a concluding chapter, a more direct, however short, tribute to her in the closing years of her life.

As a prelude, I must, at the risk of repetition, glance back to the great change brought to the three sisters by their father's death. It would have been a sad new beginning to all of us, had not the one purpose of our excellent relatives been to make the home course ever flow uniformly onwards in the same channels, *i.e.*, in ministering to the poor, in training the young, in improving cottages and land, and, throughout all, in ever maintaining, and even increasing, the outflow of family affection towards the older and younger members alike ; and, towards the younger, especially, more and more extending the hand of companionship.

In all this there was certainly no breath of change:

yet, undoubtedly, there was a difference—a spirit had departed.

There was a charm, and a great charm in the house still: yet, with the silver-toned ring of a voice, and the dignity and grace of a manner and style that were no more, a peculiar feature of that charm had assuredly departed. It had ceased to be a presence. It had been transfigured into a sacred memory.

"It was always the custom of this house." That was what Ann, the eldest of the three daughters, was ever wont to say when referring to any habit, observance, or principle of her father's inspiring.

What was "always the custom"? Especially courtesy and considerateness towards all, and particularly towards inferiors. Sunday duties—I sum up under that generality, devout worship, earnest moral and religious teaching of the young, gracious influence all around. Week-day amenities I know not how to particularize. Truly, things pure, lovely, and of good report were "the custom of the house" in the earlier days, under the courteous domination of its head, and they ever remained the custom of that house under the dutiful presidency of the daughters. I should have said the "sanctified" presidency, but for wishing not to seem extreme. But surely in filial devotion, and in God-fearing carrying out of all duty unvaryingly, unwearyingly, in all daily living, and with all kindliness and tenderness, and pleasant cheerfulness, towards all in the different relations of life—surely in these there is a true element of sanctity, if any service to God in common daily life can partake of that element.

With a great desire, I desire to render some poor tribute to my aunts for their life-long example of excellence. I am not now writing from the dear memory of youthful delight and admiration, but from the full and sober experience of age, which knows well the excellence of real goodness, and the difficulty of maintaining its unbroken course of affectionate service through all the changing scenes of life, and through all the changes of feeling towards one or other who disappoints, or thwarts, in the prolonged course.

"Begun, continued, and ended," in one true service; bearing the searching trial of continuance. Sober, just, temperate; pious, tender, gracious; in judgment discerning; in acting unswerving—who, of mature knowledge and experience, will gainsay the credit due to the gentle and honourable women who bore the distinction and the burden of ownership and leadership, through long years, without masculine assumption, or feminine weakness.

I make that last notification markedly. I have come to understand, through long observation, that leadership and ownership are impediments rather than aids to the more delicate beauties and graces of the womanly nature; and that to pass through the ordeal of change from the natural sphere of subserviency to the unforeseen height of rulership, and to lose no affection, and provoke no jealousy, from brothers, for instance, who might feel themselves superseded, or relatives, or friends, generally, betokens much, very much indeed.

"Honour to whom honour is due." And very much indeed of credit, of honour, and of affection, was the rightful due of these excellent women; and, in truth, was accorded to them, and freely and warmly so by all who knew them, but most fully by those who knew them most closely. It is touching —I may truly say it is tenderly touching—to hear, in simple language, the warm testimony of honour and love spontaneously rendered now, at this distance of time, by such few of the old sand-land stock as can speak from their own personal knowledge, and, indisputably, from their most cherished remembrance. It is but a few weeks since one of those few rustic survivors of the old patriarchal times said, in converse with my cousin, (the same to whom the earliest memories are addressed) "I often and often think of Miss Mary Formby. When I was a girl, I used to think it was worth while to try to go to heaven to be there with her." And, now, to me, it is a grave satisfaction to cast back my view over the long course of that family life my aunts so beautified, and to lay hand and seal on all I have often testified before, of the love and honour I have ever borne towards them.

This first April morning, in the early dark hours, I was meditating on many things—things concerning the course of this perplexingly intricate life, and the bearings of it towards the solemn end, and the illimitable future. As a diorama unfolding itself, the family life of the Formby home, so inseparably interwoven with myself, passed in review before me. Whence this deep impress which years and change have never lessened, and which the nearing to the end rather seems to impress more deeply? How could words and their tone, and the room in which they were spoken come, as present, to me; crossing or mingling with the most solemn approaches to the Holy and the Eternal, unless in their sweet and sober reality there was a kinship to the Heavenly?

It was that kinship to the Heavenly—I know it now—that gave that deep impress. Childhood felt it by instinct; youth and reflecting years by conviction; and, now, age, and the religious mind, recognize, and solemnly accept it.

The diorama of this early morning unfolded the living history of these successive periods; representing chiefly the later. Of that later I have written

I

less; the earlier I have recurred to again and again. This, then, is a fitting moment for aged experience to come forward, and bear its more assuredly reliable testimony to the later and more responsible epoch.

What I have now to tell of its strong claims to honour and esteem refers, in chief part, to Ann and Mary, the two eldest of the daughters; as Elizabeth, the youngest, as I have before said, died much the earliest, and her part, too, was more especially in the household direction—a less marked though not inferior office; for have we not Milton's authority to affirm, that—

> "nothing lovelier can be found
> In woman, than to study household good."

Moreover, she was not unfrequently away on long visits; and hence, taking a less active part in business matters, her greater leisure made her a very frequent visitor among the cottage people, and had even its extra share in giving brightness to the home. Still, it is of the older, and longer surviving two sisters, that I am now about to treat from the standpoint of mature judgment.

Take the decades from 1840 to 1860, though I might go several years further back. But take the two decades; twenty years is a long period for an uninterrupted continuance in a self-chosen course, devoted, "in simplicity and godly sincerity," to love and good works, beautifying family intercourse, and cementing kindly affections with the humbler classes —the poor and the afflicted especially.

One home peculiarity to be noted, in the united time of the three sisters, was the tender love and admiration that Elizabeth (Bessy, as she was always called), bore to her sister Mary, throughout life indeed, but increasingly in the more responsible years. This dear attachment and closer intercourse

A FORMBY COTTAGE.

ran along with deference more especially shewn to Ann, the eldest sister by several years. Mary also paid deference to Ann; but the bond between them was close. They were of one heart and one mind. Mary had at all times taken the more active part in the family: she had been her father's secretary; and, now, on her was laid all the active management of the property of the three. It was she who superintended the carrying out of the improvements which were devised by the two in common. Their aim was to help by giving employment. They maintained a staff of winter labourers. It was Mary's part to take the long winter walks to overlook the enlargement of the cottage, or the filling up of the turf-pit from the sand of the sunburnt meadow, which was more inclined to grow tormentil and bird's-foot clover, and the running pink convolvolus, than hay grass. To lower the level was to fertilize; and many a pleasant corner that was so dry and sandy and flower-beflecked was thus, at the cost of its flora, made profitable. And the picturesque low, thatched, and white-washed cottage called for more bedroom accommodation to promote the proprieties of family life.

That, in yielding the acting direction of all such work of improvement to the younger sister, no shade of jealousy, no interference of self, ever clouded the deep love of the elder, and less prominent, to the second and more administrative worker, may be in itself a leading tribute to the character of that elder one, whom all so honoured with a silent honour given peculiarly to herself.

And when I reflect upon the unswerving rectitude, and the depth of devotion which underlaid that quiet exterior, and gentle reticence, which loved to walk in shaded paths, I inwardly feel how just, indeed how unavoidable was that honour!

An instance occurs to me in passing—a little amusing, perhaps, but to the point. One of the brothers, and one to whom all deferred a good deal, arriving unexpectedly one day, tired, threw himself on one of the sofa couches in the North room, and told the footboy to bring him a pair of slippers. The boy did not catch the words in full, and too nervous to ask what he was in fact to bring, retired, and re-appeared with a small tray of wine and biscuits. My uncle, irritated with his blundering, spoke impatiently, and called him a fool. The boy, frightened, hurried out to repair his mistake. My Aunt Ann rose up, and, in a calm firm voice, addressing my uncle by name, said, "It was never the custom of this house to speak roughly to servants." "Ann," replied the habitually deferred-to brother, gravely, in a very gentle tone of voice, "you are quite right—I ought not to say such words." The boy shortly re-entered with the slippers. "There," said my uncle to him, slowly and markedly, "There. That will do very nicely." My uncle, my aunt, and I, were alone together in the room. For my part, I would not have missed the scene for anything. I did not know which to admire most—the one who had made the unflinching protest, or the other who responded to it with such wondrous gentleness.

But I now proceed with more direct reference to Mary, though it seems invidious to divide the sisters, since to both equally belonged "the reason firm, the temperate will," and to both the same unwearied solicitude in promoting all spiritual and temporal lines of goodness all around. Yet, as regards Mary, the additional prominence which had been given to her as joint executor of her father's complicated will, might, without going beyond ordinary family experience, have awakened some unkindly feeling, or irritation, in other family members, in the brothers, especially, who might have disliked the preference of a sister over them, and that too not the older sister either. That such disturbance of family relations did in no case result, may, in part at least, be due to the fact that she, who in the administrative line was chief of all, made herself at all times, and in all manner of ways, "the servant of all."

Perhaps I shall best account for what I have set forth, and enforce its truth by describing the character of that second sister in fuller detail; and I do not know that I can do this more fitly than by borrowing in full from another source what I have elsewhere, in part, quoted,—

> " Not hers alone the virtues that require
> Some stroke of fate to rouse their latent fire,
> —Great for an hour, heroic for a scene,
> Inert through all the common life between,—
> But such as each diurnal task perform,
> Pleased in the calm, unshaken in the storm.
> In her had Nature bounteously combined
> The tenderest bosom with the strongest mind:
> Sense that seem'd instinct, so direct it caught
> The just conclusion oft denied to thought."
> —*H. Gally Knight's " Portrait."*

Then, there was the conversational power—not of the kind that needs the stimulus of occasion, but such as flows pleasantly through the daily intercourse, giving interest to small and common things. There was the abiding cheerfulness, never clouded by temper or humours. The house was unacquainted with tempers and humours. There was the countenance so good to look upon; the sweet influence of voice—a voice which was like a sweet remembrance; and there was the manner, and the way—the way it was said: the way it was done.— It is not on paper that the interpenetrating graces can be expressed. All these things are gifts of presence. But there is a gift of absence which is the master-secret of the power of them all—the absence of self. *I*, and *mine*, were words I have no remembrance of hearing at Formby. Self was merged in the interest for others. Never was the absence of self, self-seeking, self-gratulation, self-consciousness, more the groundwork of a character than in this instance. Never was the thoughtfulness for others in all gravest, in all most trifling things, more a leading feature. Jealousy could find no standing point under such conditions. But I should be disloyal to the true principle that ruled all, if I failed to mention, though it may be for the twentieth time, the spring and watering source of it, in the deep reverent Christian faith and love which all closer familiars knew to be the key-stone of the arch. Alluding to the young—" To teach them to know their Saviour."—Does not this sentence come with a home sound, back to the only two survivors of all who closely knew the inner mind of that dear relative?

My father was courteous and affectionate to all his sisters. Like all the other brothers, he held the two oldest in especial honour. If there was any leaning towards Mary, it was only as regarded companionship. Towards Ann he felt a kindly reverence. It was to her especially that his thoughts reverted in his last short suffering hours. " I wish I had Ann's pious mind," was one of his last clear utterances.

There was the same feeling in the case of the other brothers. My Uncle Richard, "the Doctor," as he was familiarly called, if, indeed, he leaned at all towards Mary, rather paid the more marked respect to Ann. With Miles, the Rev., the co-executor, there was a tender bond with his sister

THE CLOSING YEARS

colleague. He would quote Mary with a ring of affectionate pride in the "Mary Formby says." It was like the "Brother Robert" of Accrington House. Hesketh, the Rev., indulged at times in good-natured banter in his allusions; but his mind was the same. James, the Rev., far removed by his long residence in his cure in Kent, came rarely into contact; the other brothers, being in or near to Liverpool, were continually in intercourse, dropping in frequently, for a night or more, during all their lives.

The waves of time have flowed over the sands of that calm period, and obliterated the traces of those secluded activities—most conscientious, most tender. I wish the page could give back the heart's sentiments as those lives pass before the matured judgment in the beauty of their sober excellence; in all their quiet self-abnegation, and daily service to God "in that state of life to which He had called them."

Mine is not the pen of the eulogist, but of the simple recorder in good faith. I would truthfully bring back the gentle features of the home life in a time, and under conditions, which can never be resuscitated—which are gone for ever as regards this present world. My task is nearly ended. It only remains to say how the last survivor, Mary, bore the sorrows of bereavement and solitude. Several years of that heart solitude wore on before she was released from her labour, and called to her rest in 1859, and they were years of cheerful continuance in all the family kindlinesses of the former times, and in yet more active and responsible work. She carried out the desire of her father by building the large girls' school not far from the church; and after that the church and the parsonage at Formby Point; and when I think of the quiet pursuance of these labours, and active kindnesses, in those lonely rooms in which the very atmosphere of love and appreciation ever formerly reigned, I think of it all with as much of wonder as of reverence, and not without an irrepressible sigh of sadness for that long contrast of loneliness touched upon in her own words in the letter addressed to myself, on the opening festival of the new girls' school, with which I wind up my notice of this beautiful life.

"*Formby Hall, Jan. 15th*, 1850.

MY DEAREST KATE!

I don't know whether it is best to write when the feelings have been raised beyond the common tone, but with you I may venture as you are a willing listener to tales of sand-land topics. We have to-day had the party at the School room, which was numerous beyond either expectation or invitation, but not beyond provision fortunately. The whole has gone off well, in our parlance, and in rustic words, was the pleasantest *do* they ever had. Novelty had its attraction. The rooms new, the meeting and assemblage of all ages and classes, new, the tea and coffee instead of liquor, the early hour in the afternoon, and the music, all were new. Every house sent forth its representatives, some in round numbers—and all in good humour. There were none with wrong partners, or lacking attention, but all made their way to what they liked best. The fare was substantial: two rounds of beef, a ham, pork, leg of mutton, quantities of pork pies, bun loaves, gingerbread and oranges, to suit all tastes. The boys from both schools were invited to bun and oranges, and the girls with the addition of tea. This was made in fountains, borrowed or hired from the Temperance Coffee house, and each fountain holding about twenty quarts, and the tea and coffee ready made with sugar and cream in, and drawn from the fountain at once. This we learnt from Melling School, or, I think, the tea party would have been a failure. The singing was very pleasing, and the girls looked very modest—and parents pleased. Thos. Ball and his clarionette in full requisition. 'No best dress was left at home,' yet a highly respectably clad party, not too smart. The expression on the countenances of many was indicative of the affectionate recollection of former days, whilst the young cheek had withered to almost age: in some the furrows had been the channel to many tears. Still, harmony and

THE GIRLS' SCHOOL, FORMBY.

smiles prevailed to-day. The invitations were given to all old scholars and present attendants at the school, and all whose teams had been lent; I almost think four hundred or more were present, as every room was filled. This is all matter of fact and passed over. The deep feelings I have had on opening the school lie hid, but not concealed from you. The lively feelings of thankfulness on the Sunday when it was first opened, amounted to real enjoyment, such as I had not thought to feel again. To be allowed to complete my dearest father's plan, and far more, to extend it much beyond his ideas, was delightful, and the conviction that so much good may be done to the rising generation by giving them the words of Life, now, in their young hearts. I feel I have so many advantages to work with that it rouses me beyond my present powers. Then the sweet thoughts of the beloved in bliss,—And as I take my solitary walk at early peep of winter's morning towards the Sunday School, and memory tells of the steps taken at such hours in sweet companionship, I could indulge in visions not only of the past and present,— but incline to hear the sweet accents of my now angelic lost ones singing 'Come away,'—But we must work whilst the day lasts, and then hope for re-union. I feel how much I have to do, and how many blessings to be most thankful for, though I do so bitterly feel the losses sustained. This is not to lament sinfully, but as a mortal may.

I have heard to-day from dear Annie that a new edition is ready of the sacred history which I want very much, it will be just suited for a class. The attendance the first Sunday morning was 84—many old scholars having pleasingly joined the old troop for the outset, and hundreds ought to be found. I ought to tell you, though I may weary you, that the first Sunday Lonsdale kindly came at my request that the first words in the school might be prayer. He chose very appropriate collects, and all seemed to feel the sacred impression. To-day he and his sisters were present, not for very long, but quite sufficient. They are to come and stay here whilst the parsonage house is undergoing repair, and I rejoice at the prospect, hoping this will make them feel perfectly at home here for the future. I won't write more, I am tired. Kind regards to Mr. Jacson, and most affectionate love to you.— Ever yours most entirely, M. F.

P.S.—Your pretty silk appeared in the shape of very nice bonnets over smiling faces yesterday, all as you would wish."

The last year or two of her solitary life, my Aunt

Mary suffered severely from neuralgia, and when the release came, rather unexpectedly at the very last, those who best loved her, and knew how shattering the severe suffering was, most thanked God.

The three sisters rest together with their father in the dear land of their forefathers, for which they so long laboured in love. Their graves are in the churchyard of the older Formby church; though it may seem singular that their earlier forefathers' graves are in the churchyard of the new church dedicated to St. Luke at Formby Point. That new church, built by my Aunt Mary, stands by the churchyard of the original Formby church of long past generations, preserved for a century back in but rough fashion from being wholly buried by encroaching sandhills (see p. 156); and forming at all times a point of interest for a ride on the ponies of the later era, or for a musing meditation. I add here, to bear out the illustration, one such, as it was jotted down in my last visit to it in its undisturbed and then, seemingly, abandoned solitude.

THE OLD CHURCHYARD IN THE SANDHILLS.

> A spot of such full loneliness,
> That he whose joy on earth is gone
> Might stand within its boundary lone,
> And, in his spirit's dreariness, bless
> The moment's desolate happiness.
> —Or one might seek its solitude
> In tearful meditation's mood;
> To muse on some entrancing theme,
> And weave unblam'd a daylight dream,
> 'Mid the lorn emblems, rude and grey,
> Of life's deep griefs and transient stay;
> And nought should jar—though wild and strange
> The wide expanse of sandy range—
> Upon the spirit's harmony,
> But rather soothe its trembling joy;
> The sunbeams lie so brightly there,
> So calmly sleeps the summer air,

THE OLD CHURCHYARD IN THE SAND HILLS, 1840.

MUSING MEDITATION

The desert space so freshly gleams,
And Heaven's deep blue so watchful seems,
That one might gaze untiringly
Into its depths with spell-wrought eye,
Until the heart believed its tale
That these wild lands own some strange spell,
Some love-compelling miracle;
A mystery of heart-soothing peace,
Silent as sleep in weariness.

And is it true these summer flowers
That ring their chimes to ocean winds,
Beyond all others have such powers,
Binding to love unconscious minds?
These rustling harebells, whisper they
To every ear such melody?
—And hath the glimmering atmosphere
To other eyes a charm as dear?
—Or rather, is it childhood's thought
O'er all these things the spell hath wrought,
Childhood's eye and memory,
Childhood's love and purity?
Is it the voice of early days
That lingers in the harebell's lays,
Restoring to the soul again
All that too long hath shrouded lain
Of childhood's meek unreasoning faith
In goodness, beauty,—its pure sense—
Its deep unquestioning reverence
Breathing unuttered? Untaught faith!
First blossom of the immortal wreath,
No wonder thou should'st intertwine,
In memory's meditative shrine,
With earthly flowerets bright as these,
Nourish'd by sun and ocean breeze,
Undimm'd, unsullied, scattered here
In wild seclusion. Year by year
Blooming and fading; evermore
Waving, and whispering melodies
In note and rhythm of childhood's days.
—*C. Formby, Aug.,* 1845.

Those lines were written, and the sketch taken, more than 50 years ago, and the sentiment and presence which inspired them return to me as I look them over again—the intensity of the solitude, the soothing of the silence, the depth of the overwatching blue of Heaven, and "the peace supreme." Now, there are all the surroundings of daily life—church, parsonage, residences, railway station,—the world in action. Sentiments and feelings are powerful agents in our own life, and in the world's life. Nevertheless, the practical and the profitable take precedence of them, and over-ride them in the law of Progression. My aunts had a firm foundation footing in the practical. They had a shrewd prevision of the course of progress. They foresaw the probable possibilities of the requirements of a large increasing commercial town, and in idea they pictured the villas and parades of a Bathing place, or what is now called a "Health Resort," at Formby Point, or Raven-Meols as the district was called. They pictured a church rising up in the interestingly desolate "old churchyard" in the shifting sandhills.

These things were the subject of playful talk at the tea-table. They were rebutted by the young as desecrating. The aunts smiled and chatted on. They took pleasure in the romance of the younger love; but they looked forward. I must confess they had an eye to profit. Even she, who, of all, most loved, most revered all the traces of the past; she who had described, in a whisper of reverence, the effect on her spirit of the spirit's silent communion in the soothing solemnity and calm of those "little hills that bring righteousness"—even *she*, Ann the eldest, *she*, not shrinking, but with a little flutter of pleasureable excitement, would anticipate the paved roads, and the crescents and villas we, the youngsters, deemed so execrable.

And, now, the anticipations are being realized; and a new life in a new world has been inaugurated. The rush of an alarmingly increasing population has imperiously demanded development. And since we are told, that he who makes two blades of grass grow where one grew before, is a benefactor of mankind, we cannot deny that credit to those who have made many to grow where none grew at all. At any rate these excellent ladies were not obstructives—neither were they dreamers. With their deeply religious nature they were eminently practical in good deeds, and in matters of common worldly welfare also.

But as regards the olden time, which has been the theme of the writer, the ebb-tide of receding memory is fast sweeping away even the remembrance of its customs and habits, so familiar and dear to the recorder of them. And thus it has appeared to her a work of piety to preserve to some future generations, an outline at least of the characteristics of their predecessors, under conditions foreign to what one may confidently reckon will be their own experience, but conditions which tended to foster most affectionate and most Christian-like relationships between rich and poor, landlord and tenant, cultured and simple. To them it may seem as a vision of Eutopia ; yet such a vision may perchance raise a meditative sigh, or touch a chord of affiliation in the heart of some far-off descendant, it may be in another land, my cousin by many removes. And oh, my unknown relative ! may you know how to value the inheritance of a once honoured name !

And now I close the retrospect, and the heart tenderly renders its parting homage to those quiet lives that, during long years, so unobtrusively carried on their daily service to God in the ways of

" Goodness, Righteousness, and Truth."

"THERE'S NOTHING ILL CAN DWELL IN SUCH A TEMPLE;
IF THE ILL SPIRIT HAVE SO FAIR A HOUSE,
GOOD THINGS WILL STRIVE TO DWELL WITH'T."
—*Shakespeare (Tempest).*

PART III

GENERAL SUPPLEMENTARY DETAILS

A few glances backward into the earlier history of the district and family alike, may not be amiss for future reference. Anything, however, further than a slight survey would carry me beyond my limits.

There have been changes in the inland border. The sea has apparently both encroached and receded in parts. In earlier times the place was of more public note. There was a landing-place for seafaring craft, and it had anciently a chartered market—an old cross, still preserved from decay, replaced an earlier one, said to have been a market cross.

THE FORMBY FAMILY

As regards the family itself, it is ancient, and deeply rooted in the soil; but its first origin is lost in the obscure distance. It has been a simple article of faith that it came in with the Conqueror, but direct proof on that point is wanting. The name, as Fornebei, is in Domesday Book. Very probably its origin goes further back, as the termination "bi" or "by" is said to be Danish. Evidences of proprietorship, in family deeds, remaining in preservation, date between 1200 and 1300. In the earlier deeds the name is written more akin to the Domesday form—as " Hugo de fforneby," and the like.

Though, for centuries, the only resident proprietors in the wide district, the Formbys were not the sole proprietors, the larger proportion belonging to the Blundells of Ince-Blundell—a neighbouring more inland district—the Blundells and the Formbys being conjointly lords of the manor; the latter family inheriting their share—to quote, now, from Baines—

"through an unbroken line of resident progenitors, in possession, probably, for some generations, before we find Thomas de fforneby and Alianora his wife, seized of a moiety of the manor in 1372. . . . The present joint lords of the manor, and representatives of the respective families, are T. Weld Blundell of Ince Blundell, and the Rev. Lonsdale Formby of Formby Hall."—*See the notice in full in Baines'* " *History of Lancashire,*" *ed.* 1870, *pp.* 191-2.

There is further mention of Formby Hall as "a picturesque old house of the fifteenth century, or of uncertain date, isolated and sheltered by a wood, in which a heronry still existed in the early part of this century."

Formby Hall has been found in very late years to be, in so many parts, decaying through age, that its present possessor, John Formby, Esq., has been compelled, while making some additions, almost to renew the old part; though, as far as possible, preserving its original form.

To pass on to characteristics. That the family shared in the warlike character of the early times, is to be inferred from the traditionary absolution, granted by one of the Popes to one member of it, for military service in his favour in Italy—a grace not confined to the individual himself; but extending to all posterity. That one Richard Formby, at

THE LAST HOME OF THE HERONS.

THE GRAVE IN YORK MINSTER

any rate, was of military distinction, as squire or armour-bearer to Henry IV., is beyond doubt, since his bones lie honourably interred in York Minster, behind the high altar, with the following inscription, taken verbatim from the original stone, though here rendered more legible by modernizing the lettering, and filling up the abbreviations:—

"Hic jacet Ricardus Fourmbi quondam Armiger domini nostri Regis qui obiit vicessimo secundo mensis Septembris, Anno Domini 1407. Cujus animæ propitiator Deus."

The inscription from the original stone, as above, is given in Gent's "History of York," 1730, page 132, with the following comment:—

"This gentleman lies behind the altar, near the monument of Mrs. Raines, and indeed seems particularly remarkable, as having been (as supposed) the King's squire or armour-bearer, perhaps in such a manner as the armour-bearer, mentioned in Scripture, was to the brave and valiant King Saul. If so, this Richard Formbi was armour-bearer to Henry IV., who, we read, came hither, to York, in order to proceed against his enemies in the North, and by whose command the unfortunate Archbishop Scroop lost his life, with many others."

The identical stone, placed in the Minster in 1407, is now in the porch of the lately-built Church of St. Luke, at Formby Point, having been cracked in the great fire of the Minster in 1840, and brought from thence, by permission of the Dean (after being replaced by a fac-simile), by my Uncles, Dr. Formby, and the Rev. Miles Formby. It is noteworthy that the skeleton of this royal satellite being examined during the replacing of the stone, presented a physical feature shared by some of the more recent of his name, viz., an unusual length of the thigh bone.

That learning had its due place among the family members, is evident from the notice in Foster's "County Families," that John Formby filled the office of Principal of Brazenose College in 1510.

That one or more alliances were made in marriage with a branch of the Stanley family, is shown by existing deeds of settlement, not without general interest, as evidencing at once the greater value of money, and the simpler habits of life in our forefathers' times.

AS TO ANTIQUITIES

Among so simple a population, and in a corner of the land so long removed from life's greater ambitions, few notable antiquarian remains are likely to be found. One closely concerned with the common needs of both greater and less alike, is preserved in the drawing of the old wooden mill of the district, of the time of Henry VIII., so constructed as to turn cumbrously round to meet the winds. It was taken down a few years ago by the Rev. L. Formby, in the fear it was no longer safe; but some of the timbers were found to be yet in a very sound state.

A further more mobile relic of olden pursuits and interests, was a heronry, which I can myself just remember as existing. The herons built in the old fir trees in the wood, not interfering with the rooks, whose domain was chiefly in the beeches in front of the house. The old fir trees died away one by one. The last of them is preserved in the preceding sketch, takĕn in 1844, which faithfully renders its almost every twig. Falcon perches remained in the house till lately, when they were inadvertently destroyed by workmen, unwitting of their value as relics.

CHARACTER OF POPULATION

The district was purely agricultural; its inhabitants being by nature and habit quiet and industrious, and far removed "from the madding crowd's ignoble

THE OLD MILL. (TEMPUS HENRY VIII.)

strife"; their short and simple annals offer little of mark to notice. The prayer of Agur was fulfilled among them. Neither poverty nor riches forced their respective temptations upon them. If one or two of the larger farmers were "well-to-do," none were wealthy. With most, their moderate earnings supplied their moderate wants. Holidays and excursions, or the changes of fashion in dress, were no drain upon their resources. Those temptations were unknown; and if need came through accident, or sickness, help and solace could be reckoned upon from the unfailing kindness of the one family they looked to—to them, the one source of general good in every form. And such solace was ever ready, and the needed help would be ever given—given as help, not as alms—in the form most enabling the recipients to help themselves, and most foreign to pauperizing.

There was in fact very little pauperism. The simple cottages, thatched and whitewashed, with sanded floor and little garden, had an air of comfort and cheerfulness indicative of self-respect and content, which would be very much confirmed by the manner of greeting you would receive on entering any one of them. Unquestionably there was an inherent rustic grace peculiar to this simple population. I have heard it said, and by a stranger to the place, that a Formby woman might be known in the Southport market, or elsewhere, by a certain quality of manner difficult to explain as why so distinct and pleasing. No doubt the inheritance, through long generations, of partial dependence upon and of kindly intercourse with the ruling family, had inoculated the district both with the consciousness of unfailing interest on the ruling part, and the sense of feudal or filial relationship on its own, resulting in a combination of frankness and deference in feeling and manner quite peculiar. It seemed natural to the place—it pervaded the atmosphere like the undefinable scent of the sea. One would need to coin a word to express it. In roundabout description it was a freedom of trustful homage offered on one side, and a receptive adaptability on the other, showing itself, whether in calm grave tenderness towards suffering or age, or in gentle protecting kindness towards youth or childhood. Anyway, it was a mutual relationship of receiving and repaying, in its speciality possible only in the patriarchal times which are past, and under conditions which cannot, now, by any effort be renewed. And thereupon I have felt myself called to endeavour, at least, to retain for awhile the memory of it.

I am inclined to think this feudal monopoly had much of its root in the territorial name. It has been a conjecture that the name of the Formby family was originally " De Mida," a name occurring in an earlier century, and seemingly melting away. If it had been so in fact, and the name had been retained, I doubt that the clan-like attachment would have had the same depth.

Or there may be yet a further explanation of it, in the isolation of the place—the only outlet or inlet to more general life having been, for so long, the unattractive twelve miles of hard pavement to Liverpool, unlikely to allure, unless on necessary business, rider, driver, or pedestrian. Other than that, there was no approach available to the civilized traveller. Consequently, fenced off, as was the quiet district, on the east by the broad waste of moss land, and on the wide west by the sea, one may truly say that the right of the family, who were the single source of honour and influence, to the fealty of the simple population, "there was none to dispute."

LOCAL CHARACTERISTICS

AGRICULTURE

As regards local characteristics, what I here, and indeed in all other instances, take note of, refers to the earlier part of the first half of the present century, as I have had no personal knowledge of the developments of the latter half. Arable cultivation was the prevailing rule. The land did not fatten cattle. Wheat, rye, and potatoes were the favourite crops. I may notice here that potatoes are said to have been first known in Formby; some say introduced by a Formby man sailing in Sir Walter Raleigh's expedition; others, as washed up on the shore from a wrecked vessel. However that may be, I have a strong remembrance of the handsome straight ridges of the flourishing flowering plants, alternating with fields of wheat or rye, or a rarer meadow, as we walked through each in succession, by narrow pathways, on the Sunday mile and a half way to church, morning and afternoon—if in rain, getting very wet about the dress skirts in crossing those luxuriant potato ridges, with such narrow allowance of passage—very wet, yet never muddy. I have before noted the immunity from dirt, or what in the vernacular of other places, unfavoured in that respect, is called "slutch." We passed through but few pasture fields; cottagers, and even small farmers, only too often pasturing cow, or young colt, or two or three sheep, fettered or foot-logged, in the wide, grassy sand-lanes, from whence they, not very rarely, made their way into some more fertile field, and ended in the "pinfold."

I may notice here a peculiarity, in the absence of stones. I cannot recall ever coming in contact with one of any sort. And further, there was an absence of worms—I, at least, never met with worm or grub in turning up the sand, or doing any kind of garden work. The soil was pure sand—yellow, or darkened by decayed and pulverized vegetable matter—a property more agreeable, I daresay, to the dilettante cultivator than profitable to the hard-working agriculturalist, labouring for marketable produce.

I should add, however, that one part of the district, called distinctively "The Formby Fields," was more fertile than the larger portion; and in favourable seasons could produce luxuriant crops, even of meadow grasses, annual or perennial.

THE ROADS OR LANES

The roads of the district, *i.e.*, the sandy lanes, so often alluded to, as so much contributing to the seclusion of the place, were wide. They would have been smooth lengths of flowery sod if cartwheels could have been dispensed with. As it was, three or four deep cart tracks ran in parallel lines; the two wheel-ruts, and the one middle horse track, cutting deep in the light sand, leaving the intermediate lines of green and flowery sod several inches higher. Hence, to pass from one track to another caused a heavy jolt. In the earlier times, before the invention of the convenient two-wheeled carriage, a man was employed, during the week, to smooth the way to church for the family coach, by filling the deeper ruts with sods from the raised part, and thus levelling the surface in some measure.

The moss lanes were of the same nature, only the tracks were cut through dark peat soil, instead of yellow sand. And it is worthy of notice that you stepped, without boundary mark, unknowingly, from the sand on to the moss district. That was as flat, but was altogether unmarked by the "cops" and

WILD GROWTHS

hedgerows that diversified the other; and had none of its dry and flowery pleasantness. Moreover, in winter it was sometimes impassable, whereas the sand lanes were rarely worsened by weather. The year's supply of coals for the Hall, brought by canal to Burscough Bridge, was carted over the moss, on some one-appointed summer day, by the tenantry, according to clause in their leases. It was a gala day for the household; the earliest team was decorated with ribbons, and a dinner was given in the laundry to the men in charge after the last arrival. In the farms and cottages " turf "—properly peat—was used, almost wholly, for firing, and the smell of peat smoke awakes, now, a pleasant old-world home remembrance.

It was the usual habit of farmers high up in the sand district to take their heavily laden weekly market carts, the three or four miles up to the paved road, on the Friday evening, and proceed with them the ten to twelve paved miles, early on the Saturday morning, to the Liverpool market, returning the full distance by the evening.

NATURE'S GARNITURE OF WILD GROWTHS

The wild flowers were bright and abundant, and there was much to interest the botanist. In some of the lakes, or the wet patches among the sandhills, the rare waxlike flowers of the " Pyrola " were to be seen, and even now, may be seen in abundance, and the charming "Grass of Parnassus" was (as now) scattered about in plenty, along with a variety of less conspicuous growths. A list of some fifty names, of greater or less rarity, lies at this moment before me. Amongst them, Meadow Rue, Sea Holly, Melilot, Pink Centaury, Water Violet, Evening Primrose, Yellow Wort, Sea Spurge, Bay-leaved

Willow, Hound's Tongue, Marsh Hellebore, Yellow Rattle, Purple Loosestrife, etc., etc.

The dwarf willow, with its silver-lined leaves, grew very freely among the sandhills, and on their uncultured confines; and the creeping runners of the dewberry seemed to delight in interweaving themselves with its sprays among the tangle of grasses and flowers, which made a thick, springing carpet for the foot to tread on, before it sank into the hot sand of the wilderness of little hills. The like tangle of twigs and grasses lay often as a carpet of living green beneath the clear water of those lakelets, which, sinking and re-appearing with rain or drought, were such a source of interest and delight to the lover of nature's growths, exploring in these gentle solitudes.

I allude here, as everywhere, to times very far away; but I am told that, though some of these interesting tracts of nature's garnishing have yielded to the more profitable interest of asparagus fields,* yet a large portion still remains in its natural condition, and the starr-grass waves to the sea-breeze, and the dwarf-willow, and the free growth of green carpeting, still border and line the lakelets in the miniature mountains which the sea winds have raised.

THE AVIS TRIBE

In so boundless a range of liberty over sea and land—in so wide a space, uninterrupted by mountain ridges, or canopy of smoke from town or tall chimney, even to the keen eye of the sea-bird sweeping over the shore of the unlimited sea—in such an uninterrupted range for the free wing, anyone might surmise that the avis tribe would abound

* The property mostly of my brother, Richard Formby, of Kirklake Bank, Formby Point.

THE AVIS TRIBE

in numbers and varieties. It was, indeed, so. Anything like a full treatment of this especial point of naturalist interest would carry me far beyond my bounds. Of land birds, besides the herons and rooks, there were abundance of the smaller species in the woods about the Hall, besides a variety of temporary visitors, and birds of passage, all too numerous to chronicle. Of those which haunt the sea-board there were multitudinous varieties, common and rare, all of which, in former years, had their undisturbed fishery in the sea waves, and their safe refuges on the wide stretch of rarely-trodden shore, and in the security of the sand-hill wilderness, amidst its miniature lakes and forests. The whole district, indeed, was a very royalty and sanctuary of the feathered tribe, as also were the watery wastes of the moss-lands, ever a happy hunting ground for wild duck, teal, and widgeon; shieldrake, wild goose, and lonely bittern at times—never anywhere to be found in numbers.

Interesting notes, "On the Bird Life of Formby," as now existing, have been made by Mr. J. Wrigley, a late resident, born in the place in its more recent times, from which I extract the following among the many non-universal varieties—Dotterell, Wheat Ear, Golden Plover, Quail, Water Rail, Woodcock, Snipe, Wimbrell, Coot, Water Hen, Dabchick; and, among the almost innumerable sea tribe, the Cormorant, Auk, Guillemot, Puffin, The Divers, and others not to be numbered of the Tern and Gull and Sandpiper species. The writer regretfully adds his conviction, that all these abundant varieties must die out, more and more, as the increasing population streams in. And it is a further proof of the attraction that the place has, even yet in its later years, been felt to possess, that he notes mournfully the growing disappearance of green fields, and "the replacing of the picturesque thatched and white-washed cottages by small red-brick houses, which stand glaring at one in regulation rows, where, ten years ago, was a sandy lane."

I am assured, however, by my relative, Ann L. Formby, and, by her, am begged to testify, that there still remain, yet unspoilt by the usurping hand of progress, here and there, a secluded lane, grassy and sandy, where the tormentil and pink convolvolus, the rest-harrow and heart's-ease, straggle under the foot, along the cart-tracks, and over the "cops"; and freer water-growths blossom in the damp sand of the clean ditches that skirt them.

But I have digressed far from my bird subject. A word might be added as to the multitude of young cuckoos hatched about the borders of the sand-hills, in the former days wearying in autumn with the oft-repeated note, so welcome in spring. Also as to pigeons—the large flock of the "Blue-Rocks" tenanting the pigeon-house at the Hall used to vie in their soft lulling note with the different wild species, and are still happily not decoyed by them from their tenant serfdom. I used to be told, in the young days, that the lord of the manor had alone the right to maintain a "Dove Cote," and the "Pigeon House" was ever, in dear memory, a chief adjunct of the all-pervading charm of the general earthly Paradise.

ECCLESIASTICAL

This is a large subject, and one out of which much of interest might be brought to light—and, probably, will be, as inquiries, now on foot, advance into the earlier stages of the local history.

But I can only touch lightly on probabilities, and confine myself shortly to facts. That availing researches must go far into antiquity, I infer from the derivation of the name—Formbi, we are told, being the Danish term for "Holy Place," or "Pious Place." This would imply something of the nature of consecration, or appropriation to religious rites, practices, or institutions—of what nature, originally, it would be bold to surmise, but not too bold to assume, eventually, of a Christian character.

Referring once more to Baines, he does not attempt any research into Danish times, but mentions only, that the Parochial Chapel of Formby is, in 1660, described as "ancient," and that "in 1597, Robert Halsall, vicar of Walton, bequeathed 6/8 to it." "The founder," he remarks, "is unknown."

Further, he goes on to say,

"In 1746, a brief having been obtained in 1742, for £1,154, the Church was transferred to its present position—the original site, once the centre of the village, being near the sea, was, owing to the increasing inroads of the drifting sand, left a lonely and desolate burying-ground, in a wilderness of sandhills."

Formby Church, therefore, the Church all knew, in the early half of this nineteenth century, as the one Church of the district—the Church of my grandfather, who, I may say by the way, took holy orders, at his especial personal desire, that he might constitute himself the father of his people in spiritual matters, as he was, by inheritance, in matters temporal—that well-known Church, so affectionately regarded by the old inhabitants, is not the old original, but is, in fact, only the substitute and representative of the original, which, for centuries, occupied the site of the old Churchyard in the sandhills. This peculiar fact is the source of some perplexity, and seeming contradiction, to strangers.

Having alluded to the opening of the railway in 1850, Baines adds—

"Still more recently, the sandhills, having been, in some measure, levelled and cultivated, a small Memorial Church was built in the burying-ground on the old site, by Mary, daughter of the Rev. Richard Formby, and consecrated in 1855."

This small Memorial Church has been, very lately, added to by another member of the family.

I should yet further mention that the Church, which, in the early half of the century, all knew as the one Church of the place, and, in the more recent days, as the old Church (St. Peter's)—that Church of the former generation, and of their parents, is, many hear with sorrowful regret, under sentence of destruction as "delapidated," and is to be replaced, when funds are obtained, by one, more in agreement with modern tastes, which run forcibly towards externals.

This same Church, as it stood in our own patriarchal times, is faithfully represented in the illustration. (See page 73.)

There is yet another Church, built within the last ten years, "Holy Trinity," the population being so rapidly on the increase.

I am recording, however, not what *is*, but what *was*, which is altogether a much simpler matter. Along with the one plain Church, there was, also, one still plainer Roman Catholic Chapel, the moderate population being pretty nearly equally divided between "Church and Chapel," as the phrase then went. And, very peaceably so divided; for in those much less ecclesiastically awakened days, controversial subjects, and polemics generally, were not the subjects of common converse in ordinary intercourse, and Christianity seemed to express itself sufficiently in general friendly dealing and kindly fellowship.

The Roman Catholic priest would occasionally dine at the Hall in my grandfather's time; and sorrow and bereavement ever drew forth helpful sympathy to both creeds alike, from the one leading family.

Courtesy has a large part in Christian fellowship, and is an effective antidote to religious bitterness; and the fact of courtesy having been so much a prevailing family characteristic may account for the absence of any such bitterness in the former days; and having been also a characteristic of the latest departed family representative, it may equally account for the fact that, so lately as on his death, perhaps the most touching tribute of regard and trust, among the many from all sources, paid to him (the Rev. Lonsdale Formby) was contributed by the present head of the existing Roman Catholic communion. Nor have I any reason to doubt that the old kindly fellowship continues to prevail, at least so far as the present members of the family are concerned.

In the early part of the century no other religious denomination existed. Now, not only do religious edifices multiply, but philanthropy has put forth its first embodiment in a "Home for Waifs and Strays," very recently formally opened by the Bishop of the Diocese. The Home has been built by the "Church of England Society for Providing Homes for Waifs and Strays," on a portion of the Formby estate, sold, one regrets to remember, many years ago, by a junior member of the family, and, now, in the hands of a Company.

CONCLUSION

Before I take a final leave of the singular place which has been my subject, I cast one concluding glance back towards the dim unknown of its early history. I call it a *singular* place, for is there not some singularity about it, even if we do but pass in review its changes through easily traceable times. Beginning, let us say, a few centuries ago, before Liverpool had any prominence as a seaport; probably before it had any prominence at all,—we must look with respect upon Formby as a place of some measure of public note and utility, with a landing-place and a market, with good roads, doubtless—presuming on the general estimate by which roads were reckoned then—being level, sandy, and passable in all seasons, —easily maintained, moreover, in their average availableness, by spade and grass seeds. Here we must remind ourselves that all things travelled slowly then. Progress, therefore, advancing leisurely, this condition of comparative distinction probably had a reign of some continuance.

Next, view this modest market seaport gradually falling out of notice, superseded; presently totally eclipsed, by the imperial commercial supremacy of the overshadowing merchant city—its safe sandy roadways cast into disrepute by the triumphs of pavement first, and finally of Macadam.

Now, consider, further, its geographical position, so promoting its sequestration from public usefulness, and consequently from public interest. Isolated in a corner of the land, and shut out from other populations, no thoroughfare, or passage to anywhere else, it bore a suggestive similitude to the scriptural Laish, being, as one may say, "far from the Zidonians, and having no business with any man."

Under these conditions, Formby, as a thinly-peopled agricultural district, having naturally fallen into separation from the busier world, and become concentrated in its own life, fell, just as naturally, through the attraction of interest and affection, into a dependency or environment of the one family of resident proprietors; and by the mingling ties of birth, name, and ownership, became to that family a heart inheritance, extending beyond the tie of real proprietorship.

And, truly, an inheritance of a *heart* proprietorship it may justly be said to have been—an inheritance transmitted from the older to the younger; and, by them especially, taken in all simplicity as a natural exclusive right, with which none other had—or was likely to wish to have, concern. To the general mind there may be a touch of the ludicrous, or of the presumptuous, in this idea, now; but it came quite naturally then, in the secluded patriarchal times, as a simple fact—about as simple a fact as that England was one's country.

So secluded, indeed, was the Formby district then, so little generally heard of, thought of, or known, that if the name chanced to appear in a newspaper, or in any way in print, it was as an apparition; it startled one, and raised a momentary questioning doubt whether it were a glory or an impertinence. I remember, in long past years, cutting out the printed word, and keeping it as a mixed curiosity and distinction.

Now—need I say—Now, how changed! How great a revolution, in all ways, has already come to pass—how almost suddenly come to pass, and how rapidly developing! A change in a few years into a peopled locality of divided influences, of various classes with diversified pursuits and interests, and warring opinions—a change in mutual relations, in circumstances, and in duties—a total all-pervading change.

Who shall resist the force of the inflowing tide? or who shall deprecate the irresistible? Was not almost the first impetus given to the inflowing tide of change by the re-transforming of the romantic desolation of the old churchyard, the awhile ago abandoned burial-place, so long left to the requiem of the winds among the sandy hillocks? See it, now, in the revolving changes, re-enclosed, reverently re-fitted, guarded by its again-built protecting church, the focus of a growing new population—a few still closely connected with the times of yore—but the majority altogether independent of them.

Nevertheless — nevertheless — in this impartial notice of commendable restoration and advance, may the one who records it be permitted, unblamed, to interpose, as in parenthesis, a whispered lament for that which is driven away, is obliterated, by the triumphal transformation—to interpose a whispered lament for that irreclaimable companionship of solitude, that heretofore unbroken quietude, which shrouded the long long ago, the impenetrable long ago, whose spirit, whose very presence haunted the calm desolation. Ah! be permitted one pardonable sigh for that irreclaimable presence gone—exorcised, by the modern, electrical, time-and-space-mastering activities of the present. And yet an added one, less warrantable perhaps, for the yellow untrodden, unsullied, smooth sandy surface, so pure in its spotlessness beneath the infinite overwatching depth of Blue.

CONCLUSION

How many of my friends may laughingly observe that this present moment, of all others, is peculiarly unfitted for anything approaching to a regret for the darker ages, or an incense-offering to the uncultured Byegone! But, the national exultation over all the progressive developments of this glorious reign notwithstanding, and independent of all private feeling or dear associations, and apart from all sentiment also, the old churchyard is undoubtedly a centre of much of remote interest, and, in its former strangely desolate condition (faithfully represented in the illustration, page 138, from a drawing by my own hand) very suggestive of enquiry extending a long way beyond any response I can offer.

Was indeed that Resting-Place, so long left to the guardianship of "the little hills," and the blue heaven,—that lonely God's acre, was it the resting-place where chiefly the "rude forefathers of the hamlet sleep"—they whose sons, or whose progenitors, did but guide the wooden plough that oxen drew, or who dared the sea-waves in rudely-fashioned boats as fishers—or were they, possibly, in some cases, themselves the priestly guardians of the "Holy Place," or their lineal successors? What a fund of interest would lie in a suggestive answer!

Further, I would ask, what is the explanation of that item in the marriage-settlement made by Richard Formby in 1510 regarding his "manor and *chapel* of Formby"? Does it not suggest that before the transference of the then church at Formby Point to his nearer neighbourhood, there existed some (if a private) place of worship in which he held entire or partial ownership, or patronage, independent of the more distant church or chapelry?

These are far-stretching enquiries going back into the dim times which are the province of the antiquary or the archæologist. To such I leave them, to the studious and the competent, who by science and intellect, through investigation and inference, can "by their so potent art," "call spirits from the vasty deep," and make the dead to speak.

But, for myself, I have but dealt, through less potent powers, with one long life's memories of a more recent antiquated time, yet, for all that, with a very distinct time in its seclusion and quiet, and in its long-left-behind habits of thought and mode of living. I have dealt with the simpler joys of rural life, in simpler times, and with the more scriptural forms of domestic and family relations in those times. After all, my subject is not so much in discord with the present almost world-embracing celebration of a marvellous reign; for is not that celebration in fact a tribute to the super-excellence of the womanly graces of our Queen, which have glorified it? And are not these my memories, in chief, a tribute to the blest influences of the beauty and grace of the womanly character in a different sphere? A tribute they are (I would they were of tenfold force) to the gentle influences of faith, and love, and good works, in the quiet gloaming of the still eve before the dawning day of great changes. And I offer them as a faithful portraiture of the pleasureableness and peacefulness of useful lives, spent, away from the fever of the more restless world of Progress, apart in a "Pious Place."

"Who hath despised the day of small things?"

FINIS.

APPENDIX 1

In 1910 Catherine Jacson published *'The Formbys of Formby: in temporibus paternis'*. This was a book of illustrations dedicated to her grandfather, the Reverend Richard Formby. In her Preface to the Illustrations, the author explained that most of the sketches '…were taken by myself during the latest days of the patriarchal period – say, between 1830 and 1845 – a period intimately known to myself as being that of the last closing years … of the flowery cart-track'd lanes, before the advent of paved roads, first; and, later on, that of the Railway, which, passing along the Formby coast-line, cut away its seclusion by … directly connecting Liverpool with Southport – and then going on to Preston, branching out into all the northern counties and into Scotland; thus revolutionizing all former conditions, and inaugurating the present Cosmopolitan era, which is now so quickly obliterating all realization of the former centuries-prolong'd, calmer, and more domestic life.'

A selection of these illustrations provides a fitting appendix to this centenary edition of *'Formby Reminiscences'*.

The Avenue Entrance to the Manor House in 1844

The South-eastern side, with Yew Tree

The Hall Entrance

The Narrow Door into the Garden, on the North

The Gate to the Wood

The Farm Buildings

The Granary Steps

The North End View of the Farm Buildings

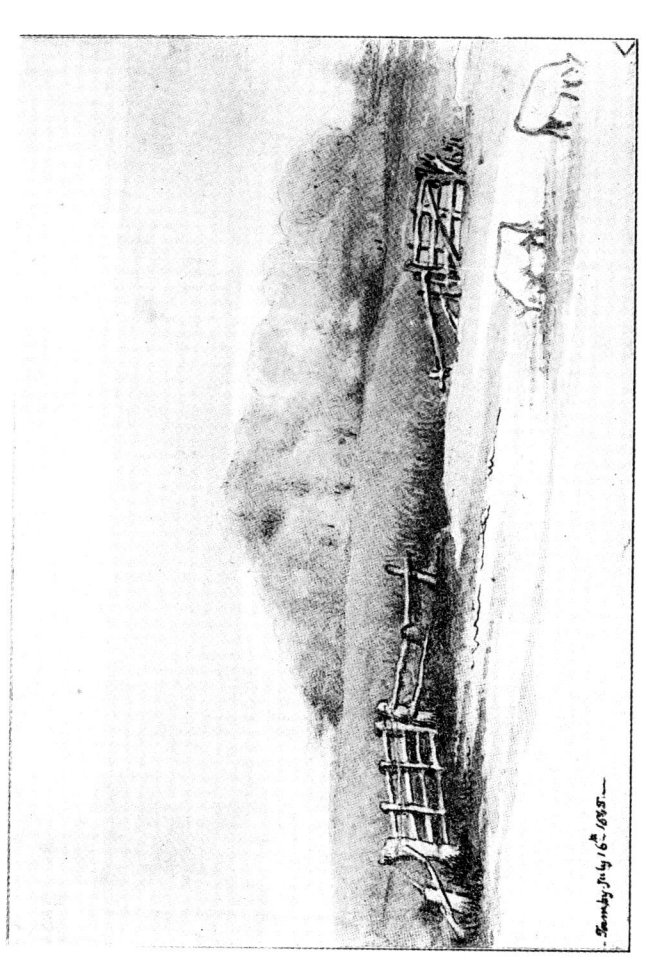

A Meadow to the Front of the Manor House

A Rustic Gate from the Wood, showing the School

APPENDIX 2

Sefton Libraries wish to thank the following Subscribers who showed faith in this special Project.

Abbeyfield (North Mersey) Society
Frank Abbott
Thomas James Abbott
B.L.Anderson
Graham Arnold
Mrs Sheila Ashton
John Bailey
Mr.L.Bailey
Dr.Martin Bamber
Mrs J.Barnes
Mrs J.Barton
Mrs G.B.Baucher
Mrs Edna Baxter
Elsie Beardsell
Michael Bedford
Jean Beer
Birkdale & Ainsdale Historical Research Society
Ewan Blackledge
June Blackshaw
Mrs Joan Bradbury
James Bradshaw
Mr. R.Breen
Mrs Patricia Bretherton
M.E. & M.L.Brian
Mrs W.Broughton
Mrs Ruth Brown
Russell Brown
Margaret Brunskill
Michael R.Buckles

Mr.R.Buckles
Mrs K.M.Bullock
B. & M.Burgess
Andrea Burton
Councillor James W.Byrne
Margaret A.Cairney
B. & R.J.Carter
Mrs Margaret Cassidy
Mrs J.C.Cawley
Ian M.Chapman
Shirley Childs
Mrs Linda Chisholm
Mr.A.E.Christian
A.E.Church
P.Clulee
Charles Collier
Rev.Paul Collins
Anne M.Connell
Margaret & Colin Cooke
Agnes Cooney
Mrs M.A.Corran
Mr. & Mrs T.Cox
Colonel Mary Creagh
Mr. & Mrs R.F.Creer
Frank Currie
Mrs Joyce Currie
Bridget, Thomas & Gerard Curtis
Ernest & Margaret Dalley
June Davies
Ellis Dean
Miss M.J.Dean
Mrs Lucy Dempsey
Mrs M.P.Dempsey
Patricia Dixon
Michael Dolan
Mrs L.M.Donaldson
Frank Douglas

Mrs Ivy Down
D.J.Duckworth
Mrs Joan Dyson
Denis East
Robert Fairburn
Mr. & Mrs J.Fenerty
Joseph Owen Fielding
Mr.J.A.Fielding
Rose Alice Fielding
Mrs D.C.Firn
Mrs E.V.Flather
J.Flatman
Francis W.Formby
Therese & Bernard Formby
Niel F.Fraser
Miss Claire Louise Gilchrist
Christine Gray
Professor T.Cecil Gray
Mrs J.Greene
A.R.L.Greenhalgh
Mr. & Mrs J.Grindle
Barbara P.Guest
Andrew A.J.Guy
Mrs Dorothy E.Habgood
Pauline Hall
Mrs P.Hasprey
Valerie Hawgood
Mr.Richard & Mrs Marion Hellam
Mrs Enid Helm
Vivienne & Gordon Hilbert
Mr.J.Hilton
Professor & Mrs Allan Hobson
Jack & Mary Hogan
Helen Holland
Maureen Hornby
Mr.G.M.Horne
Jenny & Brian Horner

Norma Horsfall
D.E.Houghton
John Houghton
Miss Alice M.W.Houghton
John Houston
Mr.Paul Humphreys
Mrs Lena Humphreys
Mrs G.E.Hutchinson
Mrs Anne Ibbs
Angela Jackson
Mr.C.L.Jaggers
John James Johnson
R.K.Johnson
Dr.Ken Jones
L.E.Jones
Ms Janet Kemp
Margaret Kennedy
Bryan Kernaghan
Desmond Lamb
Mrs E.J.Lawson
Mr.A.J.W.Leadsom
Mr.R.J.Leadsom
Mrs C.M.Leary
Mr.J.W.Leather
Canon Raymond Lee
Mrs Vera Lee
Joyce Leigh
D.V. & B.G.Levin
Councillor Pauline Leyland
S.L.Lilley
Mrs C.Lindfield
Geoffrey Lintott
Mrs J.Little
Jacqueline V.Littler
M.I.Lloyd Jones
Mrs P.A.Lockwood
Peter & Shelagh Lucas

Mrs Helen Lupton
Mr. & Mrs J.Lynes
Daphne Maher
Miss Susan E.Mawdsley
Mr.R.P.Mawdsley
Mrs M.Mawdsley
Mrs P.E.Mawdsley
F.G. & B.D.Mayer
Richard J.McCarthy
Michael McComb
Miss Sheila McGeary
Margaret A.Meadow
Mr. & Mrs J.Melling
Mrs P. & Mr.J.Middleham
Mr.C.J. & Mrs F.B.Miller
R.G.Milles
Miss I.M.Mills
Mrs R.M.Mills
Mrs M.Morley
Mrs Yvonne P.Morris
Debra L.Morton
Mr.T.Moss
Raymond Moyses
Elizabeth Murphy
Mrs E.Newell
Mr. & Mrs F.A.Noble
James William Nocton
Mr.K.R. & Mrs N.D.Owen
Jean Page
Mr.Robin Page
Joan & Barry Parkinson
Mrs M.I.Parrott
Mr.J.Paton
Mr. & Mrs M.L.Pearce
Mr. & Mrs J.N.Pennie
Meryl Petrie
Mgr. Joseph F.Phelan

Mr.R.Pickering
E.S.Pidgeon & E.M.Gardner
Colin Pierce
Janet & Roger Pontefract
D.Poole
H.E.Rawsthorne
Miss W.J.Rigby
G.W.Rodda
Mrs S.Rowe
Miss Brenda M.Saul
Mrs Nicolette Scarisbrick
Mr.D.A.Scott
Mr.J.B.Scott
Ivy Anne Seddon
Mrs D.Seddon
Sefton Professional Development Centre
Mrs Honor L.Sharp
Mrs D.Shewring
Dr.J.G.Shoesmith
Mr.Keith Smith
Mrs Edna Smith
Mrs R.F.Smith
W.A.Smith
Charles W.Southern
Jenny & Tony Stanistreet
P.Stanistreet
Patricia M.Starkey
Miss I.Stott
Mr. & Mrs Gilbert Sutton
Mrs Mary Swan
Andrew J.Swift
Michael John Swift
Mr.David Swift
Peter Nicholas Swift
Winefride Swift
Mrs E.Swindells
Mr. & Mrs J.Symonds

Mrs S.Taylor
Mrs W.Thompson
Mrs D.E.Thornton
Geoffrey J.B.Toms
Jean Toms
Tree Tops Hotel
Mrs D.Vernon
Mr. & Mrs R.R.Wagstaff
Mabel Walsh
A.Waplington
Ken & Elizabeth Ward
Mary Ward
John & Linda Warren
Derek J.Watchorn
Barbara & Bob Watts
Fay L.Watts
N.C.Webb
Jacqueline Weir
Mrs V.M.White
Mrs B.Whitfield
B.M.Whitlock Blundell
Denis Wilford
Mrs Marie T.Willett
Mrs V.Williams
Mr.C.J.Wilson
Woodlands Primary School
Alan & Margaret Woods
Mrs A.J.Wright
Mrs A.M.Wright
Mrs Gillian Wright
Dr. & Mrs R.A.Yorke
Myles Yorke & Jane Smith
Nigel Yorke & Rebecca Bridle
Yvonne Yule
Anonymous subscribers (4)